ChristLight

Reflecting the Image of Christ in the Real World

Janet T. Hoffman

Woman's Missionary Union
Birmingham, Alabama

Woman's Missionary Union
P. O. Box 830010
Birmingham, AL 35283-0010

For more information, visit our Web site at www.wmu.com or call 1-800-968-7301.

Dewey Decimal Classification: 242
Subject Headings: DEVOTIONAL LITERATURE
                  JESUS CHRIST—DEVOTIONAL LITERATURE

Cover design by Freda Souter
Design by Janell E. Young

ISBN: 1-56309-660-9
978-1-56309-660-0
W036103•1005 •1M2

Dedicated with love and gratitude

to these who reflected Christ's Light into my life

when I was a teenaged girl—

Bobbie and Scott Thompson
my parents, who prayed for me (and still do!)

Dr. Jim and Dorothy Parker
my pastor and his wife, who preached and taught God's Word

Lois Sumerlin
my missions organization leader, who modeled a gracious, giving spirit

Margie Woods
my encourager in ministry

Helen Wheeler
my example of a true witness

Contents

ChristLight . . .

Life begins in darkness. In the beginning, darkness was everywhere. *"And God said, 'Let there be light,' and there was light. And God saw that the light was good"* (Gen. 1:3–4).

Light is the highest priority—the first thing God created. Light enhances vision and awareness, provides warmth and security, multiplies possibilities and opportunities. No wonder that God made light first.

Dark is the absence of light. Darkness connotes blackness, blindness, ignorance, secrecy, and evil. Wherever Christ is not, wherever He is unknown or unaccepted, there is darkness.

Millenniums have come and gone since God created light. Centuries have passed since Jesus Christ identified Himself as the Light of the world. Still darkness prevails for hundreds of millions of the world's people who are without a glimmer of light. But we have the Light! When we know Christ personally, we have the ChristLight that takes away the hopeless darkness of sin.

Through this devotional journal, you'll be encouraged to draw closer to Christ so that His light may be reflected through you into the world. Drawing closer to Him and His light begins as your heart connects with His. You'll have daily heart-to-heart talks with God as you focus on these five areas:

"My Heart to God's" contains a teen's deep feeling or concern as she pours out her heart to God.

"God's Heart to Mine" is a verse or more of Scripture that relates to this concern.

"Heart Thoughts" are devotional thoughts, including stories of others' experiences.

"My Heart's Prayer" guides praying with thoughts, questions, ideas for application, and an opportunity for you to journal as you pray.

"Heart Blessing" offers daily encouragement and personal blessing from God's Word.

I pray that these pages will guide, inspire, and challenge you to draw others to His love light as you:

reflect with Christ through prayer;

reflect on Christ through Bible study;

reflect Christ's light by sharing your blessings;

reflect Christ's light through ministry and witness; and, ultimately,

reflect Christ's light in the world.

Janet T. Hoffman

Reflect with Christ Through Prayer

Day 1

My Heart to God's

I want to know You better, God. I've learned from experience that if I want to build a relationship with someone, I must be willing to spend time with that person. So if I truly want my relationship with You to grow, I must spend time with You. The problem is that I never seem to have enough time. That's why I've decided to use this devotional book as a daily guide. Help me to stick with it, not to let what my friends think I should do, my up-and-down feelings, or even doing good things keep me from spending time with You each day. I really do want to grow closer to You.

God's Heart to Mine

"As soon as Jesus was baptized, he went up out of the water. . . . And a voice from heaven said, 'This is my Son, whom I love; with him I am well pleased.' Then Jesus was led by the Spirit into the desert . . . fasting forty days and forty nights" (Matt. 3:16 to 4:2).

Heart Thoughts

Jesus understands your problem. He, too, desired a close relationship with the Father. Yet He had to deal with what others expected Him to do, plus His own human emotions, and never enough time to do all the good things He saw to do. His answer was to make time with God His number one priority.

Jesus' baptism was an important experience in His life, as it marked His connection with us and the beginning of His mission for His Father. This was a time of commitment for Him—a public commitment to do the task God had sent Him to do. As He realized that He would need time alone with God in order to prepare for His job, He withdrew to the desert wilderness to spend 40 days praying and fasting.

If 40 days in a deserted place was necessary for Jesus, God's Son, to prepare for God's plan for Him, do you and I need the same? Are you willing to commit a few minutes daily for the next 40 days to be alone with God in a quiet place, focusing only on Him and His plan for you?

My Heart's Prayer

Thank You for coming to live on earth so that people like me can relate to You.

Lord, if You needed 40 special days to concentrate on God and His plan for You, then so do I.

Realizing that You have a plan for me, I commit myself to spend a quiet time with You in prayer these next 40 days. Help me to focus totally on You and to be completely honest with You. Make a difference in me, Lord. As I spend this time with You each day, make me more like You.

This is my heart's prayer today, Lord (write your own prayer thoughts below): _____

_____

_____

Here is my commitment. I'm willing to set aside _____ minutes each day to spend in quiet time with You, God. My commitment for 40 days begins on (month)_____ (day)____, (year)_____, and will end on (month)_____ (day)_____, (year)_____. My quiet time will begin at _____ (A.M. or P.M.). My quiet place is _____.
Signed _____

Heart Blessing

"'You will seek me and find me when you seek me with all your heart'"
(Jer. 29:13).

Day 2

My Heart to God's

Having good relationships isn't easy, is it, God? It's easier to do all the talking, to tell what I want and why, and to control the conversation. Listening—really paying attention to what someone else is feeling as well as saying—is hard. But if I want someone to listen to me, then I guess I must be willing to listen, too.

Is the same true for a strong relationship with You, Lord? Each day I'll tell You what I'm thinking and feeling, what hurts me, and what brings me joy. And then, am I to listen? Am I to just shut out everything else and focus on what You want me to know about You? To be honest, God, I'm not sure how to do that.

God's Heart to Mine

"'This is My Son, whom I love. . . . Listen to Him!'" (Matt. 17:5).

"Be still, and know that I am God" (Psalm 46:10).

Heart Thoughts

Do you live in the fast lane? Want fast food, fast computers, fast bikes, and fast cars? Don't want someone slow to get in your way?

God says, "Be still!" That's the first step in listening to Him. He doesn't just mean, "Be quiet." He also means, "Give up. Stop. Loosen up."[1] Give up your own thoughts, your selfish ideas, your wants, and your worries. Stop thinking about yourself for a while. Loosen up! You can relax in God's loving presence. He cares about your every thought and feeling.

"Know that I am God." That's the second step. "Know" means personal acquaintance with God's presence.[2] To know Him is to experience His love firsthand and to invite Him to take control of your life. When you know Him like that, you can trust Him in times of trouble or fear. You'll never be alone again.[3]

9

Want to listen to God? He says, "'*Step out of the traffic! Take a long, loving look at me, your High God*'" (Psalm 46:10 *The Message*). Listen by reading His Word, hearing words of a worship song, or being sensitive to His still, small voice within.

Without a doubt, God is speaking. Are you listening?

My Heart's Prayer

Thank You, God, for caring enough about me to listen to me. Help me to listen to You, too. In order to hear what You want me to know about You, I'm willing to give up, stop, and loosen up.

I understand that a personal relationship with You is more important than anything. Though I don't deserve it, I accept the gift of Your love for me. I don't want to be alone. I want You for my friend, my boss, and my helper.

This is my heart's prayer today, Lord (write your own prayer thoughts below):

I need to give up: _____

_____

I need to stop: _____

_____

I need to loosen up by: _____

_____

I need to know this about You: _____

_____

(Talk to a trusted Christian adult about this if you need additional help.)

Heart Blessing

"'*Call to me and I will answer you and tell you great and unsearchable things you do not know*'" (Jer. 33:3).

Day 3

My Heart to God's

OK, God. I've realized the need to set aside time each day to talk (and listen!) to You. I've made a commitment, and I'm doing my best to keep it; but I need more help understanding what is involved in real prayer. Sometimes I hear adults pray using old-fashioned words like "Thee" and "Thou." Those prayers seem fake. Nobody talks like that anymore.

But when Mrs. Chapman, my youth leader, prays, I get the feeling that something more is going on. She seems uniquely connected to God. Her prayers seem real.

I wish I could pray like that. Who can teach me?

God's Heart to Mine

"One day Jesus was praying in a certain place. When he finished, one of his disciples said to him, 'Lord, teach us to pray'" (Luke 11:1).

Heart Thoughts

My high school English teacher combined teaching English literature with writing. After we studied a special kind of poetry, I hurried through my writing homework (to write a sonnet) in order to do something I liked better. When my teacher read my poem, she said, "You have a good idea. But you did not pay attention to my instructions, and you did not follow the pattern of the master writer. You'll have to do it over."

A successful student pays close attention to the teacher. When the disciples felt like you do, they asked their Teacher, Jesus, "Teach us to pray." What we call the Lord's Prayer is the model Jesus gave in response to their request (see Luke 11:2–4).

If we pay careful attention to the Teacher, we'll discover that real prayer is based on God's greatness and our needs.[4] First we must recognize the greatness of God. Jesus began His prayer doing this. His prayer opened by calling God Father, indicating the intimate relationship they had. Then Jesus gave honor to the very name of God, acknowledging God as ruler of the heavenly (spiritual) kingdom.

Real prayer begins with praise and thanksgiving for God's greatness. Praise Him by honoring His name! Thank Him by listing what He has done for you! Try praying an entire prayer of thank-you without asking God for anything. Then as you go through the day, thank Him silently each time you are aware of another of His blessings.

My Heart's Prayer

Thank You, Father, for Jesus' Model Prayer because it teaches me how to pray. Thank You for being willing to be connected to me through prayer. Please help me to pay really close attention to Who You are and to how great You are. Help me to give honor to You each time I pray. Remind me that Your plan for me is more important than my own.

Today, as I think about You, I'll list here some names that tell of Your greatness (for example: Creator, heavenly Father, King of kings): _____

_____

_____

Thank You, God, for all the things You provide for me and do for me each day. Today I want to give my special thanks for these things:

_____

_____

Heart Blessing

"Know therefore that the Lord your God is God; he is the faithful God, keeping his covenant of love to a thousand generations of those who love him and keep his commands" (Deut. 7:9).

Day 4

My Heart to God's

I like spending this time with You each day, God. I find myself thinking more about You all day long when I begin the day with You. I was surprised yesterday when I began listing all the things You've provided for me. I've been thinking ever since about Your greatness, something I learned from Your Model Prayer.

But isn't there something more I should learn from that prayer? Besides talking about You, there's plenty in that short prayer about "us." Does that have anything to do with me?

God's Heart to Mine

"'Give us each day our daily bread. Forgive us our sins, for we also forgive everyone who sins against us. And lead us not into temptation'" (Luke 11:3–4).

"If we confess our sins, he is faithful and just and will forgive us our sins and purify us from all unrighteousness" (1 John 1:9).

Heart Thoughts

Lauren was visiting at our house. Our two-year-old granddaughter took her granddad by the hand and led him to the kitchen. Still holding his hand, she pointed up to the cabinet where she remembered that cookies are kept.

"I want sumpin'," she said. She was definitely hard to resist, but her granddad told her that she should wait since it was almost time for a meal.

"But, Pappy, I *need* sumpin'!" she begged. This tiny toddler had already discovered that need is more important than want.

After we express adoration for God's greatness, we admit our basic needs. Not our wants, but our needs. Jesus' teaching prayer spells them out. Physically, we need food to exist and we need it every day. Powerless to produce it or to earn it without the help of

God, we are to acknowledge that God is the One Who provides nourishment.

Spiritually, we need forgiveness of sin. Sin is doing what I want to do instead of what God wants; and God's Word says, *"All have sinned"* (Rom. 3:23). We also need the power to say no to temptation. No one is strong enough to do that without God's help.

Real prayer—like little Lauren's plea—declares our needs and connects us to the only One Who can meet them.[5]

My Heart's Prayer

You are truly all-powerful, God. In Your presence I am so aware of my own weaknesses. Help me to be totally honest as I admit all my needs and failures to You.

Though I'm getting stronger as I mature, I lose energy quickly if I go too long without eating or if I fail to eat healthy foods. I can't think clearly then either. Those things remind me of how I must have food to do my best physically and mentally. Help me correct unhealthy eating habits by:_____

_____

_____

I have spiritual needs today, too. I need your forgiveness for these things I've done:_____

_____

_____

And please forgive me, Lord, for failing to do these things I should have done: _____

_____

Give me the courage and strength to say no when I am tempted to do these things: _____

_____

Heart Blessing

"Then you will call, and the Lord will answer; you will cry for help, and He will say: Here am I" (Isa. 58:9).

Day 5

My Heart to God's

I'm feeling down, God. My good friend Sara is going through a rough time. Her mom is really sick. Doctors are testing for cancer, and Sara is scared. Some guys I looked up to at school have started drinking. Amanda's in lots of trouble with her parents because she stayed out past midnight last weekend. Ashley's family is moving next week, and she wants to stay here. And Andy brags that he's not a Christian.

I want to help my friends, but what can I do? I can't control others' decisions, much less their diseases. All of this is absolutely frustrating.

God's Heart to Mine

"If you are having trouble, you should pray. And if you are feeling good, you should sing praises. If you are sick, ask the church leaders to come and pray for you. Ask them to put olive oil on you in the name of the Lord. . . . If you have sinned, you should tell each other what you have done. Then you can pray for one another" (James 5:13–14,16 CEV).

Heart Thoughts

Have you listened to a child pray lately? Marie's bedtime prayer is a roll call of people she knows and loves: "God bless Mama and Daddy, my big sister and baby brother, Mamaw and Papaw, Granny Bea, Mrs. Gray (baby-sitter), Cindy (playmate)," and on and on she goes.

Young Jack offers to pray at the end of the pastor-led children's time during Sunday worship. His prayers go something like this: "Dear God, please make my granddad remember to take his medicine, 'cause he's really sick. Help my brother to make a good grade on his spelling test tomorrow. And help Johnny to quit pickin' on me just 'cause he's bigger."

No wonder Jesus said we should become like children. Children pray for the people they care about. And Jesus modeled praying for others (also called intercession). He was always praying for others—for those who were sick, those whose loved one had died, those who were hungry, those who needed understanding, those who were His enemies, and even for you! (Read His prayer for you in John 17:20–24.)

Interceding for others in prayer is asking God's very best for them. You might try doing this while walking down the halls at school or through your neighborhood. Call it prayerwalking. However you do it, pray for others!

My Heart's Prayer

O God, thank You for caring so much about me that You prayed for me! I'm learning so much from the ways that You prayed. Because I do want Your very best for my family members and friends, I'm going to pray for them just like You prayed for Yours. I admit that I have enemies, too. I'll even try to pray for them, but I'm really going to need Your help with that!

I'm listing here the names of the people I'm praying for today and the reason each needs prayer. (I'll put an asterisk [*] by the names of people I consider enemies.)

<u>Person</u>   <u>Prayer Need</u>

_____   _____

_____   _____

_____   _____

_____   _____

_____   _____

_____   _____

Heart Blessing

"The prayer of an innocent person is powerful" (James 5:16 CEV).

Day 6

My Heart to God's

I'm stressed out, God. Besides praying for my basic needs and other people, there are lots of other things I care about but can't handle.

The pressure is worse sometimes than others, but it's always there. There's the tension of wanting to obey my parents, yet wanting my independence. Or trying to make good grades, yet not having time to do everything my teacher requires. Or wanting to be heard, yet feeling that no one understands when I speak. Or wanting to keep my body pure, yet having a crush on a guy who drinks and likes sex on dates. Or wanting to stand up for You, yet yearning to be accepted by the crowd.

Do you care about these things, God? Is it selfish to pray for myself?

God's Heart to Mine

"He began to be sorrowful and troubled. Then he said to them, 'My soul is overwhelmed with sorrow to the point of death.' . . . He fell with his face to the ground and prayed, 'My Father, if it is possible, may this cup be taken from me. Yet not as I will, but as you will'" (Matt. 26:37–39).

"Cast all your anxiety on him because he cares for you" (1 Peter 5:7).

Heart Thoughts

During one of my most stressful times, my friend Ann gave me a book of prayer poems by Ruth Harms Calkin. I still find great encouragement in this one:

> O, dear God—
> It comes to me
> With sweet and gentle relief
> That this thing in my life
> Which I can't possibly handle

Is the one thing above all
That You *can* handle.
You can handle it totally
And You can handle it now.
"Yes, dear child—
Now let Me!"[6]

Jesus knew stress. When He was a youth, His parents didn't understand Him. When He left home to begin His ministry, His family felt forsaken. Even when He became popular for miracles of feeding and healing, people wanting His favor wouldn't give Him a moment's peace.

His disciples often disappointed Him and eventually betrayed Him. He was ridiculed, spit upon, whipped, and crucified for a crime He did not commit. Yes, Jesus knew stress. And when His cares weighed heavily on Him, He prayed. By His example, He teaches us that praying for ourselves is not just OK; it is essential!

The key is "Thy will be done." Pour out your heart to the Father. You can trust Him to do what is best.

My Heart's Prayer

How could I doubt that You care? Thank You, God, for sending Jesus to live on earth so that He understands exactly how I feel. I want to bring to You every concern, big or little, through prayer. I'm encouraged because I believe that You can handle what I cannot. And even if the way You handle it is not what I'm hoping for, You know best. I'm trusting You to do what's best for everyone.

I'll write down the things that are getting to me right now. You do what's best.

"Yes, dear child—now let Me!"

Heart Blessing

"The Lord is good, a refuge in times of trouble. He cares for those who trust in Him" (Nah. 1:7).

18

Day 7

My Heart to God's

You've already answered my prayers for a few things this week, Lord. But most of the things for which I prayed haven't changed. As far as I know, nobody has every prayer answered. I can't help thinking, *Do You hear all my prayers?*

I suppose You might refuse to answer a few things just because You can see a bigger picture from Your heavenly viewpoint than I can from mine on earth. Still, when I ask for things that I know are good, sometimes You remain silent. That's when I start to wonder: *Are You always listening? Are You really able to answer? And if so, why don't You?*

God's Heart to Mine

"This is the confidence we have in approaching God: that if we ask anything according to his will, he hears us" (1 John 5:14).

Heart Thoughts

On Shelda's sixth birthday she received a small bicycle. When she started first grade a few weeks later, she begged to ride her new bike to school. "Please," she pleaded, "let me ride it today. I'm a big girl now. Please, may I? Pleeeeeze?!"

Although our daughter's school was only two blocks away, traffic was heavy. She was a big girl compared to her younger brother, but she seemed very small to us.

"Not yet," her dad answered gently, "because some driver might not see you. We don't want you to get hurt. You must wait." (Our child wasn't the only one with tears in her eyes!)

God hears us when we pray; but He does not always respond as we expect.[7] Sometimes His answer is, "Yes, I thought you'd never ask!" Other times His answer may be, "No, My child, I don't want you to get you hurt." (Maybe He has tears in His eyes, too.)

But often His answer is, "Wait." When God is silent, it doesn't mean He's rejecting you. It may mean He's still listening.[8] If you are tempted to take matters into your own hands or to give up, remember: You never get behind when you wait on God!

My Heart's Prayer

How blessed I am to be Your child! Though more and more I feel like an adult, maybe nobody is, from Your point of view. Thanks, God, for assuring me that You are always listening—and answering, one way or another.

I think You must love to say yes.[9] Thank You for saying yes so often to my prayers. Since I'm beginning to understand that You sometimes say no because You know what's best for me, thanks for even that.

As for "Wait," now that's not easy. I need lots more patience.

Here's my prayer for today:

_____

_____

Please help me to be grateful for these yes answers:

_____

_____

Help me accept in faith these no answers:

_____

_____

And give me patience, God, for these things on the "wait" list:

_____

_____

Heart Blessing

"Then you will call upon me and come and pray to me, and I will listen to you" (Jer. 29:12).

Day 8

My Heart to God's

I'm beginning to understand how to connect with You through prayer, dear God. And I'm excited to realize that even someone like me can have a real person-to-person conversation about Your greatness and my needs.

But it's still kind of hard for me to talk to someone like You about all of my everyday problems. After all, You are the One Who made the universe and sent Your Son to be my Savior. I mean, I'm a little out of my comfort zone here. When will I ever feel more at ease praying to You? And how will that happen?

God's Heart to Mine

"'So I say to you: Ask and it will be given to you; seek and you will find; knock and the door will be opened to you'" (Luke 11:9).

Heart Thoughts

Growing up, I always wanted to play the piano; but we didn't have one. After I married, we moved next door to a piano teacher who offered to give me lessons and to practice on her piano.

After a few months, I actually learned how to play some hymns. But the most important lesson Mrs. Black ever taught me was this: To do something well, one must practice, practice, practice!

Though I had imagined learning to play a new song each week, that's not the way it happened. I was to begin my daily practice by playing scales for at least 30 minutes. Then I'd practice the song she'd assigned for 30 minutes more. "Practice makes perfect," said Mrs. Black, "so practice, practice, practice."

Prayer is like that. After Jesus gave His Model Prayer, He told a story of a next-door neighbor who knocked at the door at midnight. Needing bread to feed his guests, the man kept knocking until his friend opened the door. Because he kept on and on, the man on the inside finally got up and gave him what he needed.

That story (Luke 11:5–8) was Jesus' way of saying, "Don't give up praying. Keep it up. Practice, practice, practice." In other words, just do it!

My Heart's Prayer

Lord, when I think about Your life on earth, I remember that You prayed a lot. You were always slipping off to pray in some quiet place while others fished or ate or slept.

I want to be obedient, God, and I want to grow more like You. But I don't always feel like praying. Would You help me? Help me to pray whether I feel like it or not. Teach me to pray especially when I don't feel like it. You know better than I the reasons why I have found it hard to pray. Help me not to waste time thinking why it's hard for me. Instead, help me be obedient to Your command to keep on asking, seeking, and knocking through prayer.

From the depths of my heart, here's my special personal prayer for today: _____

_____

Heart Blessing

"*Before they call I will answer; while they are still speaking I will hear*" (Isa. 65:24).

2

Reflect on Christ Through Bible Study

Day 9

My Heart to God's

I'm not always in the mood for reading, God. I like to be more active. I know the Bible is Your Word, and reading it is one way of listening to You. But it's difficult for me to sit still for very long to read, especially if the plot's not full of action. To be honest, the Bible seems like a history book written long ago, and things have changed so much since then. I need something that grips me, that relates to the twenty-first century, and that will make a difference in my life. Can the Bible do that?

God's Heart to Mine

"For the word of God is living and active. Sharper than any double-edged sword, it penetrates even to dividing soul and spirit, joints and marrow; it judges the thoughts and attitudes of the heart" (Heb. 4:12).

Heart Thoughts

Nikolai was freezing. The Russian, having been captured and brutalized by the Germans in World War II, had vowed to find and kill the enemy soldier who savagely mistreated him. Now in a refugee camp, he searched for something to burn for warmth. Snatching paper scraps swirling in the wind, he saw words in Russian, his native language. On the torn pages Nikolai read: *"I stand at the door and knock. If anyone hears my voice and opens the door, I will come in and eat with him, and he with me"* (Rev. 3:20).

Falling to his knees, he trusted Jesus. When he stood, all hatred was gone from his heart. Nikolai was a new person!

Soon Nikolai read a Bible cover to cover. As he read, God called him to a lifetime of service. Instead of taking a life, he taught students about eternal life through Christ. And it all began with a scrap of God's Word.[1]

God's Word is powerful! If you are seeking to become a Christ follower, reading His Word will lead you to faith in Him. If you have trusted Him as your personal Savior, His Word will guide you as you serve Him. What a difference His Word makes!

My Heart's Prayer

O God, truly Your Word is powerful! I confess that I've never realized how much difference Your Word can make in a person's life.

From now on, I plan to give Bible study a higher priority in my life. I trust You to speak to me through Your Word, to make a definite and noticeable difference in my life.

Some areas of my life where I need You to make a difference are (write here): _____

_____

_____

Heart Blessing

"But you must never stop looking at the perfect law that sets you free. God will bless you in everything you do, if you listen and obey, and don't just hear and forget" (James 1:25 CEV).

Day 10

My Heart to God's

I feel so silly, God. I don't mean in my classes at school. Even when I do well in school, I seem to say silly things or make silly choices. I want to say and do the right things, but too often I mess up totally. I just don't have wisdom.

I want to grow more like You, since You always said and did right. I wish I knew how a simple young person like me could become wise like You.

God's Heart to Mine

"If you accept my words and store up my commands within you, turning your ear to wisdom and applying your heart to understanding, . . . then you will understand the fear of the Lord and find the knowledge of God. For the Lord gives wisdom" (Prov. 2:1–2,5–6).

Heart Thoughts

Bill was only 2 the first time he tried on his daddy's cowboy boots. Watching him try to walk in them was hilarious for us, but he was serious. Many times after that, I saw him walk behind his father, literally trying to step in his footprints. Bill wanted to be just like his dad.

If you want to be wise like Jesus, try following in His steps. Pay attention to how much Jesus' words and actions on earth stressed the value of Bible study.

Even as a boy of 12, He sought out Temple teachers on His first trip to Jerusalem in order to study their teachings about Scripture and to ask questions.

Throughout His adult ministry, the wise Jesus depended on and referred to Scripture. When Satan tempted Him after His baptism, Jesus responded three times by quoting Scripture. Jesus taught that whoever practices and teaches the commands in God's Word will be called great in God's kingdom. He quoted from the Old Testament while teaching the deeper meaning of the Ten Commandments and how to apply them. He read and quoted from Isaiah 61 while attending the synagogue in Nazareth.

By His words and by His life, Jesus proved the wisdom of studying God's Word.

Want wisdom? Follow His example.

My Heart's Prayer

You are all-wise, God. Forgive me for paying too little attention to Your Word.

I do want Your wisdom, God. I should have known it doesn't come overnight.

I want to seek wisdom in the right place by reading Your Word every day. Help me to take to heart what I read in Your Word, and to tune my ears to Your wisdom as I read.

Please give me the courage to follow Jesus' example by depending on Your Word for guidance as I make choices. I need Jesus' kind of wisdom to know what to say, when to say it, and when to be silent.

Special needs in my life for which I need wisdom right now are these (write here): _____

_____

_____

Heart Blessing

"The law of the Lord is perfect, reviving the soul. The statutes of the Lord are trustworthy, making wise the simple" (Psalm 19:7).

"'He will teach us his ways, so that we may walk in his paths'" (Isa. 2:3).

Day 11

My Heart to God's

I'm trying to be faithful in reading Your Word, God. But the Bible is a real struggle for me to read. I don't always know the words I read. Your Book is sometimes just way over my head. Besides not being able to pronounce the names, I have a hard time understanding the meaning of the words. So I lose interest quickly, and my mind wanders. How useful is the Bible when I can't understand it? Today I need help understanding Your Word.

God's Heart to Mine

"The Holy Scriptures . . . are able to make you wise enough to have faith in Christ Jesus and be saved. Everything in the Scriptures is God's Word. All of it is useful for teaching and helping people and for correcting them and showing them how to live. The Scriptures train God's servants to do all kinds of good deeds" (2 Tim. 3:15–17 CEV).

Heart Thoughts

A girl who was visiting in her preacher granddad's home asked him why Bible reading is so important. "The Bible . . . is God's Word," he said reverently. "It is one of God's favorite ways of speaking to us. . . . But unless folks read it, it can't do them much good." When the girl admitted the Bible was hard for her to understand, he said, "That's when different versions can help you." Later he added, "Reading God's Book is as important as eating. You must do it every day. You can't grow up as a Christian believer without reading God's Word!"[2]

I was that girl. Granddad taught me these hints for developing the habit of daily Bible reading:

- Read God's Word every day in order to know what God is like, and how to please Him.

- Choose a translation of the Bible that is easy to understand.
- Read a few verses early in the morning. After thinking about what you read, decide what you will do to apply what you learned.
- "Choose at least one verse to memorize each week."[3]

God uses His Word to shape us for the tasks He has for us. What could be more important?

My Heart's Prayer

Bless You, Father! You not only listen to me when I pray, but You also talk to me through Your Word, the Bible! Forgive me for neglecting to read it. Help me develop and continue the habit of reading a portion of Your Word every day. Give me the patience to find other Bible translations at a church media library or community library in order to understand better. Teach me at least one new thing from the Bible each day; then encourage me to apply it while it is still fresh on my mind.

I plan to cultivate the spiritual habit of daily Bible study by reading a few verses each day from the Bible Book of _____ during my quiet time with You. After reading 2 Timothy 3:15–17, and after thinking about these verses, this is what the Scripture verses mean to me: _____

_____

This is how I plan to apply it in my life today:_____

_____

_____

Heart Blessing

"Blessed is the one who reads the words of this prophecy, and blessed are those who hear it and take to heart what is written in it" (Rev. 1:3).

Day 12

My Heart to God's

My feelings are like a roller coaster, Lord—up one day and down the next. When things have been going well for me at school, church, and with my friends, reading my Bible makes me feel even better.

But things aren't always so great. Sometimes I'm lonely because I've been excluded from a group at school or because no one seems to really understand me. Sometimes I'm sad because a friend or loved one is very sick, or because someone I trusted has disappointed me. Sometimes I'm afraid because I'll soon be an adult on my own and deep down I'm not sure I'm ready, or because of frightening wars or threats of war in our shrinking world.

On days when I'm lonely or sad or afraid, I need encouragement. Can reading Your Word really help me?

God's Heart to Mine

"For I am the Lord, your God, who takes hold of your right hand and says to you, Do not fear; I will help you" (Isa. 41:13).

Heart Thoughts

Your feelings are very real, and you're entitled to them. As long as you live, there will be times of sadness, disappointment, and fear. Each of these may seem magnified if you feel excluded, with no one to share your heart's hurts. Loneliness can make everything else feel worse.

A great Scottish missionary to Africa, David Livingstone, endured serious illnesses, disabling accidents, severe hardships, and separation from family and friends in order to share the gospel with people who never heard of Jesus. When he returned to Scotland after 16 years, he was invited to speak at Glasgow University.

With his body withered by 27 fevers and his arm dangling uselessly after being mangled by a lion, Livingstone told the students: "Shall I tell you what sustained me during the hardships and loneliness of my exile? It was the promise of Jesus, 'Lo, I am with you always, even unto the end of the world.'"[4]

Where did Livingstone find Jesus' promise? In God's Word (Matt. 28:20). At every stage of life, in every circumstance, God is faithful to offer assurance, encouragement, comfort, peace, and hope through His Word—especially when you're at "the end of the world!"

My Heart's Prayer

You are wonderful, God! Thank You for always being there for me, whether I'm up or down or somewhere in between.

Some things (or persons) that have disappointed me lately are:

_____

Nagging fears that seem to keep haunting me from time to time are: _____

_____

I feel especially alone when: _____

_____

From now on, when I'm feeling all alone in this world, please remind me of this: You've given me Your Word that You're right there with me, even at the end of my rope of safety and security. When I'm afraid, I'll remember Your Word saying, "I, *your God, have a firm grip on you and I'm not letting go. I'm telling you, 'Don't panic. I'm right here to help you'*" (Isa. 41:13 *The Message*).

Thank You, God. I'm counting on Your Word.

Heart Blessing

"*'Peace I leave with you; my peace I give you. I do not give to you as the world gives. Do not let your hearts be troubled and do not be afraid'*" (John 14:27).

Day 13

My Heart to God's

I'm here again, Lord, needing Your help. A couple of weeks ago I'd never consider discussing this with You. But now that I feel much closer to You, I feel I can tell you whatever I'm thinking.

As I'm growing up, I'm getting mixed signals about my body. My leaders at church say to take care of one's body by eating right and resting; and my youth leader often speaks of keeping one's body sexually pure. But sometimes I wonder: If rich foods and drinking are so bad, why do some Christian adults indulge? Also, I have strong feelings about guys—especially good-looking ones—and I want them to like me. I have girlfriends who say that if you want a guy to like you, you have to be willing to give your body to him.

How is it possible for a girl like me to stay pure?

God's Heart to Mine

"Young people can live a clean life by obeying your word. I worship you with all my heart. Don't let me walk away from your commands" (Psalm 119:9–10 CEV).

Heart Thoughts

When Kerri was asked by a popular guy to go to the prom, the butterflies in her stomach went crazy! Although admired by many, he had a bad reputation for drinking and dropping girlfriends after he got what he wanted. Kerri replied, "I'll let you know."

"What should I do?" she asked her friends.

Several said, "Go with him, Stupid!"

Her youth leader and her mom said, "Be careful whom you date, or you'll be sorry."

God says, *"Your body is sacred . . . not some piece of property belonging to you, but to Me. Let people see Me in your body behavior"* (1 Cor. 6:19–20 The Message, author's paraphrase).

As Kerri decided what to do, she remembered her True Love Waits[5] promise to abstain from sex until after marriage. Does that mean she shouldn't say yes to the guy of her dreams?

To be like Christ is to be pure. Our world is polluted with impure lifestyles on television, the Internet, magazines, and in lives of some people we know. In order to guard our hearts and minds against impure thoughts and actions, we must spend time with God and His Word. Have you spent enough time with Him to be protected from the sinful influences surrounding you?

My Heart's Prayer

I'm glad I asked, Lord. Regardless of what anyone else says or does, I want my body to be fit for Your use.

I choose purity not just because I know there are lifelong consequences to impurity but also because I love You. Guide me to make choices that honor You, choices that will bring positive attention to You. Help me to keep my inner longings in check. When I'm about to be swept off my feet, give me courage to avoid situations in which I'll be tempted to conform to others' selfish wishes.

To be pure, I need to stop these activities: _____

_____

I need to avoid these places: _____

_____

I need to spend less time with these persons: _____

_____

I need to spend more time with these persons: _____

_____

Each time I'm tempted to make a bad choice, remind me of these words from Your Word (write out the words to 1 Cor. 10:13 or James 1:12): _____

_____

Heart Blessing

"Blessed are the pure in heart, for they will see God" (Matt. 5:8).

Day 14

My Heart to God's

Is memorizing Your Word important, God? I'm working hard to discipline myself to pray and to read the Bible daily. But my Sunday School teacher and youth leader stress the importance of Scripture memorization. I don't understand why.

Memorizing takes so much extra time, Lord. And while it may be easy for a few, most people I know find it difficult. I already have to memorize lots for school. (I don't always see the point in that either.)

As long as I'm reading Your words to me each day, isn't that enough? I just don't understand the value of learning word for word. What difference will it make?

God's Heart to Mine

"I have hidden your word in my heart that I might not sin against you" (Psalm 119:11).

"Let the word of Christ dwell in you richly" (Col. 3:16).

Heart Thoughts

When Jesus was 12, learning and understanding the Scriptures was so important to Him that He spent extra time with the Temple teachers. Later, when tempted by Satan to sin, Jesus refused by quoting Scripture from memory. His example speaks clearly!

Kathryn was 12 when a rare illness resulted in her failing eyesight. Doctors said she could lose all vision. Since God's Word was first in her life, young Kathryn's greatest concern was that she would no longer be able to read her Bible. She memorized as many Scripture passages as possible before total darkness set in.

Thankfully, the doctors were wrong. God miraculously preserved her sight. He also preserved her memory. Years later, Kathryn Carpenter often quoted from memory great passages of Scripture learned as a girl. God's words came alive as many were touched to win the world for Christ! Today she and many others continue to be blessed by the Word that she hid in her heart.[6]

God's Word stored in us is valuable when we are tempted and when others need a blessing. The best hiding place is in your heart.

My Heart's Prayer

Oh yes, Lord! I want Your Word stored in me. I need to be able to recall words from You when I'm in trouble and don't have my Bible with me. I want to know Your words by heart each time I am tempted to sin. I want to keep Your Word with me always, not only to bless my life but also to touch the hearts of others for You.

To further develop the habit of memorizing Your Word, this week I will memorize this verse (write the words to Col. 3:16 here):

_____

_____

Each time I am tempted to sin against You, I will repeat these words (write the words to Psalm 119:11 here): _____

_____

_____

When a friend needs encouragement, I'll quote my favorite Bible verse: _____

_____

_____

Give me courage to use what I've learned by heart to keep myself pure and to be a blessing to others.

Heart Blessing

"Heaven and earth will pass away, but my words will never pass away'" (Mark 13:31).

Day 15

My Heart to God's

I'm actually beginning to look forward to this time each day when I read Your Word and pray, God. But just when it seems I'm making a little progress in knowing You and trying to follow Your example, I see someone at church who is light years ahead of me in becoming more like Christ. I have to wonder: *Will I ever be like that? How? And how can I know if I'm making any progress?*

God's Heart to Mine

"But grow in the grace and knowledge of our Lord and Savior Jesus Christ. To him be glory both now and forever! Amen" (2 Peter 3:18).

Heart Thoughts

Our children had a "growing-up wall" in the doorframe of our kitchen. Here we marked each child's height as a birthday was celebrated. With bare feet and heels pressed against that wall, Shelda, Bill, and Jeff would stretch every muscle to make the new mark as high as possible. Then we'd get out the yardstick and measure. Between birthdays, the children often stood by those marks to see how much they had grown. We couldn't see much difference from day to day. But it was amazing how much each grew in a year.

Do you wonder if you are growing as a follower of Christ? Keeping a journal is a great way to measure such growth. As you write your heart's feelings during your daily quiet time, or note Scriptures you read and what they mean to you, or write your prayers to God (and His answers!), you are keeping a record of your spiritual growth. When you look back at the journal later, you'll smile as you see how God has worked in you to help you grow more like Him.

Journal your journey with God. Even if only a few words a day, it's a great way to measure how your faith is growing.

My Heart's Prayer

Lord, I don't want to stay a baby Christian. I truly want my faith and love for You to keep growing. Maybe keeping a devotional diary of my experiences with You and Your Word will encourage me to grow.

Actually, I've already started journaling by writing a few words in this book for the past 14 days. (Note: Look back now at notes you've written since beginning these devotionals.)

I think I'm beginning to grow, God! Here are my thoughts as I looked over my notes: _____

_____

_____

Help me grow more like You, Lord. And help me to develop the habit of jotting down my thoughts and feelings during these 40 days so that I may keep journaling—and growing—in the future.

Heart Blessing

"We ought always to thank God for you . . . because your faith is growing more and more, and the love every one of you has for each other is increasing" (2 Thess. 1:3).

Day 16

My Heart to God's

Lord, I think I am growing! As I looked over what I've journaled in this book, I realized my priorities are beginning to change.

Take the value of Bible study, for example. Reading Your Word is more important to me because I know the Bible has power to make a huge difference in my life.

Whenever I feel at the end of my world because I'm lonely or sad or afraid, You're holding my hand, offering hope through Your Word. By making choices according to Your Word, I can keep myself pure in the midst of temptations. By memorizing Your Word, I can resist temptation and keep Your wisdom with me no matter where I go.

More than ever, I treasure the Bible, Lord. I want You and others to know how much I value Your Word. What's next?

God's Heart to Mine

"Do not merely listen to the word, and so deceive yourselves. Do what it says" (James 1:22).

"Your statutes are wonderful; therefore I obey them" (Psalm 119:129).

Heart Thoughts

The first time a Chinese young woman held a Bible in her hands, she trembled with excitement. "When do I have to give this back?" she asked.

"This is yours. You don't have to give it back," replied her friend. Tears rolled down the cheeks of the new owner of God's Book.[7]

When a missionary to Bosnia gave an elderly woman a Bible in her language, she said, "I heard about this Book when I was a girl, and I waited all my life to see one."[8]

To these women, God's Book is priceless! What do you suppose *they* will do with it? Most likely they'll read it, then do what it says.

If you truly value God's Word, that's what you do—make sure you read His Word daily. Then do what He says. Regardless of how much you claim to love the Bible or how you talk about its importance, the proof is in the doing.

Be careful not to just let His Word go in one ear and out the other. It won't do you much good unless you act on what you learn! God wants you to apply His Word to your everyday life.

So what's next? Do what He says!

My Heart's Prayer

I get the message, God. Like those women in other lands, I truly believe the Bible is the most precious Book of all. It is so because it is Your message to me! I'm amazed that in Your Word You give guidance which is for my own good, that You want the very best for me; yet You don't force me to obey. The choice is mine.
I commit myself to be a doer of Your Word, not just a hearer. So when I read, "*Honor your father and mother*" (Ex. 20:12), I'll (write your own answer):_____

_____

When I read, "*Love your enemies and pray for those who persecute you*" (Matt. 5:44), I'll: _____

_____

And when Your Word says, "*Do to others what you would have them do to you*" (Matt. 7:12), I'll do my best to: _____

_____

I'm counting on You to help me *do* Your Word, Lord.

Heart Blessing

"*Now that you know these things, you will be blessed if you do them*" (John 13:17).

3

Reflect Christ's Light by Sharing My Blessings

Day 17

My Heart to God's

Lord, I feel so blessed! I just want to keep this kind of nearness to You so that I can be more like You. The more I talk to You in prayer and listen to You by reading Your Word, the more I feel close to You. I want to do what You say because You've done so much for me. How can I express my thanks to You? How do I respond to Your generous blessings?

God's Heart to Mine

"'I will bless you; . . . and you will be a blessing. . . . And all peoples on earth will be blessed through you'" (Gen. 12:2,3).

Heart Thoughts

Suzy developed the habit of daily prayer as you are doing. She felt as you do, absorbing the blessings of God's closeness. As Suzy talked to God each day, her prayers included many requests for His special favors. But one night she had a new insight and closed her litany of requests by praying, "And now, God, what can I do for You?"[1]

Suzy has the right idea! Prayer and Bible reading are crucial to a believer's daily life in Christ. But if you stop there, you won't make much difference with your life. You'll just be a taker. To make a real difference, you must be a giver.

Everything belongs to God. He blesses us not because of who we are but because of Who He is. We are blessed as God entrusts to us things of value. He intends for each of us to use our blessings wisely to bless others.

After soaking up (taking) God's blessings in your quiet time, splash them out on others (giving). How? By being trustworthy and responsible with what God gives you—your time, your talents, your treasure, your influence—your all.

43

My Heart's Prayer

Now that I think about it, God, I've been enjoying Your blessings without giving much in return. I do want to respond to You out of my thankfulness for all the blessings You keep pouring on me. And I definitely want to use my blessings to bring blessings to other people.

Thank You, Lord, for trusting me with Your blessings. Give me wisdom to identify my blessings so that I can use them to bless others. Help me to discover what to share and with whom.

Three blessings for which I'm especially grateful are:

_____

_____

Three ways I can share these blessings with others include:

_____

_____

Three persons I know who need a blessing are:

_____

_____

Lord, make me a blessing to someone today!

Heart Blessing

"Every good and perfect gift is from above, coming down from the Father of heavenly lights" (James 1:17).

"Guard the good deposit that was entrusted to you—guard it with the help of the Holy Spirit who lives in us" (2 Tim. 1:14).

Day 18

My Heart to God's

God, as I look around my church and my school, I don't recognize many who seem to be givers. Most of my friends (including adults) appear more like takers. Could it be that taking is human nature and giving is God's nature?

Being human, it's much more natural for me to take than to give. I do want to make a difference with my life by being a blessing to others. If only I knew a good example of a supergiver, I might be more consistent in my own giving. Would You please bring to my mind someone who models giving like You give?

God's Heart to Mine

"'For God so loved the world that he gave his one and only Son, that whoever believes in him shall not perish but have eternal life'" (John 3:16).

Heart Thoughts

Jesus was a giver. He gave His time. Jesus gave time learning the Scriptures and worshiping. He spent time with His disciples, friends, children, outsiders, outcasts, and whoever needed encouragement.

Jesus gave His talents. He used His gifts of teaching, preaching, and storytelling to illustrate God's truth and call people to Him. He used His gift of healing to bring renewed strength, and miracles to feed hungry multitudes.

Jesus gave His treasure. We can be sure that Jesus tithed.[2] A devout Jew, He knew Scriptures commanding tithing, and He kept the law perfectly. He praised the Pharisees for giving the tenth;[3] and He commended giving taxes to Caesar and offerings to God, as well as giving to the poor.

Jesus gave His influence. He invested His influence in relationships with family and friends at a wedding; His disciples by the Sea of Galilee; and close friends Lazarus, Mary, and Martha in their home. He influenced followers and critics, saints and sinners, even thieves on the cross.

Jesus gave His all. His Father loved the world so much that He gave His best: His only Son. And Jesus voluntarily gave His life that we may know the blessing of eternal life. His example challenges us to be a blessing by giving. What will you give?

My Heart's Prayer

Wow! What a great giver! Thank You, God, for giving the best Gift, Jesus. And thank You, Jesus, for modeling a lifetime of giving. I'm challenged, that's for sure.

I want to accept the challenge of Jesus' example today. While I know I can never be just like Him, I'll set some goals for giving in the same ways Jesus gave.

Time: Today I will give ___ minutes of my time to _____ who needs a blessing.

Talent: Today I will use my talent of _____ while I am _____.

Treasure: Today I will set aside $_____ of my allowance/earnings for You. (I'll give it next Sunday at church.)

Influence: Today I will use my influence with _____ to point her (or him) to You.

Help me, O God. I want to give away my blessings like You did so that more people may receive Your gift of life.

Heart Blessing

"I give them eternal life, and they shall never perish; no one can snatch them out of my hand" (John 10:28).

"Thanks be to God for his indescribable gift!" (2 Cor. 9:15).

Day 19

My Heart to God's

I'm still thinking about Your Gift, God—Your indescribable Gift—Jesus! I want to be a giver like You are, a giver like Jesus. But really, who could ever come close to giving a gift like You gave? Or like Jesus gave? Or like You keep giving to me day by day?

Any way I look at it, my attempts to respond to You are so tiny by comparison, they are embarrassing. Perhaps if I had more to offer, I wouldn't feel this way. Does the size of the gift indicate how grateful is the giver's heart?

God's Heart to Mine

"'I do not judge as man judges. Man looks at the outward appearance, but I look at the heart'" (1 Sam. 16:7 TEV).

Heart Thoughts

A woman named Mary gave costly perfume worth nearly a year's income.[4] Instead of washing Jesus' feet with water, she lavished her perfume on Jesus' feet and dried them with her hair. The disciples saw her gift as wasteful. But Jesus called her demonstration of gratitude "a beautiful thing" (Mark 14:6).

A widow gave two mites, worth a fraction of a penny.[5] Hers was a small gift, something of little value to most people. But it was valuable because it was all she had. Though others likely made fun of the size of her gift, Jesus saw it as the greatest gift that was given that day.

A boy gave his lunch. The two fish and five rolls made a great picnic for a growing boy. Andrew wondered, *"'How far will they go among so many?'"* (John 6:9). Jesus saw the boy's willingness to share. And with Jesus' blessing, the lunch fed thousands.

Just as Jesus acknowledged Mary's expensive gift and the widow's sacrificial one, and as He multiplied the boy's gift, He will take what we offer and make it more than we can imagine. It will be immeasurably more because it will point the way to Christ, Who gave His all.

My Heart's Prayer

Lord, I'm more like the boy with the lunch or the widow with two tiny coins. I don't have much to offer. But I'm beginning to understand that You look at people and gifts much differently than I do.

I wonder how the boy felt when You used his loaves and fish. Besides having plenty to eat, he must have felt thrilled that You chose his lunch! And the widow must have been overjoyed hearing Your words! To receive and give Jesus' blessing is the best gift, isn't it?

Help me to be less concerned about what others give or think I should give. Make me more concerned about what You think.

Of all the blessings You've given me, what I value most is
_____ because
_____.

As an expression of my gratitude and love, I'm willing—eager, even—to give my _____ to You, Lord!

Heart Blessing

"'Give, and it will be given to you. A good measure, pressed down, shaken together and running over, will be poured into your lap'" (Luke 6:38).

"'Remembering the words the Lord Jesus himself said: "It is more blessed to give than to receive"'" (Acts 20:35).

Day 20

My Heart to God's

I'm still thinking of how I want and need to reflect Your light by blessing others, God. But as usual, I always seem to be pressed for time.

Although it's hard for me to have daily quiet time, I'm really trying. I just don't have enough time to do everything. It takes time to do my assignments at school, time for my chores at home, and time for church activities. I need some time for me and my friends, too.

Does it take much time to be a blessing to others? And how much difference does it make to spend time being a blessing?

God's Heart to Mine

"There is a time for everything, and a season for every activity under heaven: a time to be born and a time to die, a time to plant and a time to uproot" (Eccl. 3:1–2).

"Remember your Creator in the days of your youth" (Eccl. 12:1).

Heart Thoughts

Sharon's special missions project was spending time with a nursing home patient for several months.

Once a week she visited Miss Pearl, an amputee with no hands. Sharon read Bible verses to Miss Pearl, brushed her hair, fed her, and wrote letters for her. In a way, Sharon's hands became Miss Pearl's hands.

When Sharon's family moved to another town, she made one last good-bye visit. Miss Pearl said, "Thanks for making me want to live again. Even old folks like to be loved!" Sharon made a difference by giving the gift of time.

As someone said, "People who care about us spell love TIME." How we spend our time indicates what matters most. Helen Fling shares advice she received from her mentor, Mrs. J. M. Dawson: "There will be many bids for your time. It becomes a sin not to choose the best."[6]

Time equals opportunity to bless. God has entrusted to each person 24 hours a day. Demonstrate your appreciation for God's blessings. Reflect Christ's light by making time choices that make a difference to others and bring Him glory!

My Heart's Prayer

I guess I've never thought of time as a gift from You, God. Instead, I've just thought about how there never seems to be enough of it.

Since You are the One Who made 24-hour days, and You know what things are most important, then surely there must be exactly enough time to do what matters most. The bottom line is, I need to take a closer look at my priorities as I plan my time.

Two things that take much of my time are: _____

_____

Two things that are a waste of my time are: _____

_____

Two important things for which I never seem to have time are:

_____

Here's my plan to make wiser use of my time in the next month:

_____

Help me daily, dear God, to better use my valuable time.

Heart Blessing

"Be very careful, then, how you live—not as unwise but as wise, making the most of every opportunity" (Eph. 5:15–16).

Day 21

My Heart to God's

God, why is it that some people have several talents while others have few or none? I once heard someone say, "When the Lord passed out talents, I was absent." Sometimes I feel that way too, especially when I compare myself to Stephanie who writes beautiful poetry. Or to Terri who sings like an angel. Or to Elizabeth who speaks in public with ease.

I don't mean to complain. I can do a thing or two fairly well. But there are more things that I'm unable to do well. I can't help wishing that my abilities were as special as some of my friends' gifts are. And I wonder, Lord, am I just as responsible for my talents as they are for theirs?

God's Heart to Mine

"God has given different gifts to each of us" (1 Cor. 7:7 CEV).

"Each one of you has been blessed with one of God's many wonderful gifts to be used in the service of others. So use your gift well. . . . If you have the gift of helping others, do it with the strength that God supplies. Everything should be done in a way that will bring honor to God because of Jesus Christ" (1 Peter 4:10,11 CEV).

Heart Thoughts

My mother is a great example of using one's talent. As I was growing up, Mother had no money of her own. With little education, she felt that she had no skills either. But she could sew!

Mother saved pennies from the grocery money till she had enough to buy a fabric remnant. After spreading out the material and pinning to it a well-worn pattern, she knelt over it and prayed.

"Lord," she'd say, "I'm making this for a child who doesn't have a dress for church. I can't afford to make a mistake because I can't buy more material. Please help me do my best. And use this dress to let Betsy and her mama know somebody loves them. Amen." Mother gave the gift of her talent.

Talents are among the blessings entrusted to us. Not all persons have equal abilities. Some people are multitalented, while others are single-talented. But each has a talent. To identify your gift, ask your pastor, youth leader, peers, or school counselor what they have observed. The results may surprise you. When you've discovered your giftedness, thank God for His blessing. Then explore ways to use your gift to bless others.

My Heart's Prayer

I've never thought of the responsibility that comes with blessings, God. I haven't thought much about talents as blessings either. And I never realized that every follower of Christ has at least one gift to use for blessing others.

Please help me with this, God. It's definitely easier to identify someone else's talent than to discover my own. I'll write here the one or two talents I think You have given me: _____
_____
Later today, after I ask my friends what each considers my talent, I'll write the answer here: _____
_____
I'll also ask the school counselor to share the results of my most recent aptitude test, and I'll write that here:_____
_____
My research shows that my strongest ability is: _____
_____

God, give me the grace to use this talent to bless someone today, I pray.

Heart Blessing

"And God is able to make all grace abound to you, so that in all things at all times, having all that you need, you will abound in every good work" (2 Cor. 9:8).

Day 22

My Heart to God's

I feel guilty, Lord, when the pastor preaches on giving. After all, I don't have much to give; and the few types of jobs I can get don't pay well. Even if someone would hire me and pay minimum wage, I doubt if I could fit a regular job into my schedule.

I do give a dollar on Sundays. Usually I give to the offerings for North American and international missions, too, and sometimes to state missions. But my youth group usually has a fund-raiser for those, or my parents may give me money for the offerings. So why do I feel responsible, God?

God's Heart to Mine

"A tithe of everything . . . belongs to the Lord; it is holy to the Lord" (Lev. 27:30).

"'Do not store up for yourselves treasures on earth. . . . But store up for yourselves treasures in heaven. . . . For where your treasure is, there your heart will be also" (Matt. 6:19–21).

Heart Thoughts

Seventeen-year-old Julie is a high school senior. Last year she baby-sat for months in order to buy her senior ring. Just when she had earned the last dollar needed to place her order, Julie's youth leader issued this challenge: Give a sacrificial gift to the Lottie Moon Christmas Offering®!

Julie had already given to her church a tithe (10 percent) of her earnings weekly. She knew that an offering is a gift beyond the tithe. What could she sacrifice?

When she prayed about it, she knew. Julie sacrificed her senior ring. She gave the money instead to the Lottie Moon Christmas

Offering for International Missions. In order to reflect Christ's light in the world's darkness, Julie gave the gift of her treasure!

Money is another blessing entrusted to us. Perhaps the reason you feel responsible is because you are. According to Malachi 3:8, failure to give tithes and offerings is robbing God! God has made us caretakers of His world. Seeing Him as owner and ourselves as managers makes it easier to give the tenth.[7]

Our responsibility doesn't end there, however. Spending the remainder wisely means giving faithfully, spending conservatively, and saving consistently.[8] By carefully managing the money God trusts to us, we are able to bless others in our church, our community, and our world.

My Heart's Prayer

With the privileges of growing up, I'm to be more responsible. Right, God? My responsibility is less about how much I have and more about what I do with what I have.

In order to follow Your requirements for my money blessings, I need to evaluate my personal finances. The total amount of money which comes through my hands weekly (by allowance and/or jobs) equals $_____.

Ten percent of this amount is $_____. This is the amount God expects me to give through my church.

The remaining 90 percent equals $_____. Of this amount I plan to save 5 percent ($_____) for missions offerings and 10 percent ($_____) for future plans. I pray that I may use the rest wisely.

This is my commitment, God, because I want my blessings—including my money—to bless others in Your name.

Heart Blessing

"'Bring the whole tithe . . .' says the Lord Almighty, 'and see if I will not throw open the floodgates of heaven and pour out so much blessing that you will not have room enough for it'" (Mal. 3:10).

Day 23

My Heart to God's

My teacher said that every person influences at least seven others all the time. Is that true, Lord? I know that there are people whose influence has had an impact on my life. And I can think of several who influence me now in different ways: my parents and grandparents, my boyfriend, my youth leader, and my best friend.

But when I try to think of seven people who might be affected by what I say or do, I can't. I'm not even sure that I want to influence them because that's a lot of responsibility. What if I lead them in the wrong direction?

What about influence, God? Does everyone have it? If so, how do I handle mine? Is influence a blessing or a curse?

God's Heart to Mine

"You are like light for the whole world. . . . Make your light shine, so that others will see the good that you do and will praise your Father in heaven" (Matt. 5:14,16 CEV).

Heart Thoughts

The airplane sped into the twilight sky as I dreamed of being reunited with family. Suddenly, a huge jolt awakened me. A thunderstorm tossed our plane, lurching in every direction in night's blackness. Stunned by terror, shocked passengers braced and prayed for survival. Finally we emerged from the clouds. Applause and cheers erupted as we saw airport lights beam below, leading the way to safety!

As those lights guided through the stormy darkness, Christ's followers are to shine through life's storms with the reflection of His light.[9] Our light is to draw attention not to us, but to God.[10]

Christ's radiance in Meredith is lit by His presence in her heart.[11] Never snobbish, she treats others with consideration. She doesn't laugh at Jay's dirty jokes, use foul language, or cheat at games. Meredith refuses temptations to drink or date guys with a bad reputation. Though some avoid her, she encourages often with smiles and praise. With Christ's help, Meredith's influence is showing His way to others.

Influence is a blessing from God. We are responsible for using influence to reflect Christ in every relationship. The world needs guiding lights: believers who point the way to Christ. How brightly are you shining?

My Heart's Prayer

My light is more like a candle than an airport beacon, isn't it, God? As Jesus invested in His disciples through day-to-day listening, laughing, and learning, guide me to use the blessing of influence wisely too.

Thank You for blessing my Christian life through these persons:

_____

I intend to express to them my personal appreciation this week by:

_____

Lord, I know people who need to experience or deepen their relationship with You. Realizing that my influence is a blessing for which I am accountable, I will intentionally invest in starting or strengthening relationships with these persons: _____

_____

Help me reflect Your light into others' lives today, I pray. Amen.

Heart Blessing

"Jesus . . . said, 'I am the light of the world. Whoever follows me will never walk in darkness, but will have the light of life'" (John 8:12).

56

Day 24

My Heart to God's

How rich I am in blessings, Lord! You have blessed me by entrusting me with time, at least one talent, some kind of treasure, and influence through friendships. Now I'm learning how each of these blessings comes with the responsibility to use it wisely in order to bless others by pointing them to You, God.

I want to develop the habit of expressing my love to You, reflecting Your light as I share each blessing. Looking at my journaling in this book the past week, I see ways to apply what I've learned about taking care of all You've trusted to me. And now, Lord, is there any other way that I may express my love and gratitude to You?

God's Heart to Mine

"'Love the Lord your God with all your heart and with all your soul and with all your mind and with all your strength'" (Mark 12:30).

"Praise the Lord, O my soul; all my inmost being, praise his holy name. Praise the Lord, O my soul, and forget not all his benefits" (Psalm 103:1–2).

Heart Thoughts

A child fidgeted as the offering plate was passed up and down the church pews. When the plate came closer, he became more restless.

"What's bothering you?" whispered his mom.

"I have no offering," he answered.

Soon the offering plate was in his hands. He placed it on the pew, sat in it, and said, "I don't have money, but I want to put me in!"[12]

Ralph Waldo Emerson said, "The true gift is the gift of thyself."[13] Giving to God is not just about time or talents or money. Giving to Him means offering all we are.[14] Our heart, or emotions, indicates how we feel. Our mind determines how we think. Our strength refers not only to physical fitness but also to strength of character.

Our soul is our spiritual life, determined by whom or what we worship. Giving oneself to God means surrendering all of these to Him as an expression of our love for Him.

Simply put, we turn over our life to Him, giving up control of all of it.[15]

My Heart's Prayer

Lord, all I have and all I am are microscopic when compared to Your gifts for me. In fact, as long as I'm in charge of everything in my life, it amounts to very little. But I believe that in Your hands, little can become much.

So I want to say, as Jesus did, *"Not as I will, but as you will"* (Matt. 26:39). You take control. Some specific problem areas which I give over to Your control I'll journal below.

Within my heart (emotions)—I'm having trouble with these feelings: _____

_____

Within my mind (thoughts)—I need help with these recurring thoughts:_____

_____

Within my strength (body and character)—I need to develop this healthy diet or exercise habit: _____

_____

And to work on this character trait: _____

_____

Within my soul (spiritual life)—Please stretch my faith as You help me daily give over control of my whole self because I love You, Lord.

Heart Blessing

"No eye has seen, no ear has heard, no mind has conceived what God has prepared for those who love him" (1 Cor. 2:9).

4

Reflect Christ's Light Through Ministry and Witness

Day 25

My Heart to God's

Dear God, I'm so grateful for the deepening relationship I'm experiencing with You. As I'm learning to express my gratitude to You by being a giver of blessings instead of just a taker, I feel even closer to You. I especially love the feeling that comes when You shine through me in my relationships with others. So I want to do more, God. Are there other ways that I can reflect Your light to others?

God's Heart to Mine

"Suppose a brother or sister is without clothes and daily food. If one of you says to him, 'Go, I wish you well; keep warm and well fed,' but does nothing about his physical needs, what good is it?" (James 2:15–16).

Heart Thoughts

Taylor and her mom attended their first National Acteens Convention (NAC) in Nashville. (Acteens® is a missions organization for teenaged girls.) Between NAC activities they met a sad-looking woman with missing teeth. As they visited, they discovered that the woman with no smile had severe mouth pain requiring dental attention. Taylor's mom wrote down the woman's name and offered a prayer for her.

"Can't we help her?" asked Taylor when the woman was gone. Her mom reminded her that they were already late to the next NAC event and they'd soon be leaving town. Taylor replied, "Isn't missions what Acteens is all about? I think we should put feet to our prayers!"

Within hours, they began to collect donations from other Acteens to pay for a dentist. Excitement for the "Tooth Lady" project continued after the Acteens returned home and the fund continued growing. Today the woman has a pain-free mouth and a beautiful smile—all because girls chose to demonstrate love.[1]

Ministry is love in action. "People don't care how much you know until they know how much you care," said Abraham Lincoln.[2] Through ministry you display how much you care.

Do you care? Prove it!

My Heart's Prayer

God, You have demonstrated Your love for me in many ways, such as:

_____.

Thank You for showing how much You care.

Reading James 2:15–16 really had an impact on me. I'll read it again in a different contemporary translation, and write here what it says to me today:

_____

_____

This could be a description of me, God. I've seen people dressed in rags and I've said, "God bless you," instead of giving a jacket I don't often wear. I've seen half-starved people on the street holding an "I'm hungry" sign and I've mumbled, "I'll pray for you," instead of returning with a hamburger. I have:

_____

_____.

People can't really hear about Your love while they're shivering and their stomachs are growling, can they? Forgive me, Lord. When I see a person in need today, would You remind me of this Scripture verse? And then would You love through me?

Heart Blessing

"'And if you spend yourselves in behalf of the hungry and satisfy the needs of the oppressed, then your light will rise in the darkness, and your night will become like the noonday'" (Isa. 58:10).

Day 26

My Heart to God's

"Love in action"—that's an accurate description of You, God. It seems like You were always doing ministry of some kind or other. From my perspective, that's a little confusing. After all, You are the King of kings and the Lord of lords. Shouldn't people be ministering to You, instead of the other way around?

Help me to understand this, dear God. How is it that You spent so much of Your time ministering to others?

God's Heart to Mine

"'Whoever wants to become great among you must be your servant, . . . just as the Son of Man did not come to be served, but to serve, and to give his life as a ransom for many'" (Matt. 20:26,28).

Heart Thoughts

Service, or *ministry*, has many meanings. In tennis, serving is putting the ball into play. In dining, service is hot food and cloth napkins. In church, a service is congregational worship. But to Jesus, serving means caring for another's needs without being acknowledged, doing things that don't count with men but count everything with God.[3]

Jesus Christ served others, choosing as His symbol not a scepter, but a towel and pitcher. Usually a servant washed guests' feet as each arrived, since sandals offered little protection against dusty roads. Having no servant, Jesus and the disciples must have shared such duties. At the Last Supper, Jesus humbly did what none of them offered.[4] He washed their feet. Then He said, *"I've laid down a pattern for you. What I've done, you do"* (John 13:15 *The Message*).

Christ modeled a servant spirit when He touched the leper, spoke with the woman at the well, took time with children, or touched the dead. Jesus served as He taught in synagogues and preached the good news of the kingdom. Throughout His ministry Jesus met physical and spiritual needs by giving Himself away.

Servanthood demonstrated Christ's love to the world of His day. Nothing less will win our world to Christ. It's your serve now!

My Heart's Prayer

I never thought of ministry and witness as being a servant, Lord. Thank You for showing us how we should serve. I do want to follow Your pattern—to serve by giving myself away to others as You did.

As I read the account of Jesus' washing the disciples feet in John 13:1–17, reveal to me the deeper meaning of serving. I'll write my thoughts about the passage here:

_____

Ordinary things like a towel, pitcher, and sandals remind me of Jesus' servant actions and attitude.[5] Ordinary things like _____ might represent ways I may demonstrate a servant's attitude and behavior. I can "wash feet" by:

_____

_____

With Your help, God, today I will look and listen for ways to serve others.

Heart Blessing

"What you are doing is much more than a service that supplies God's people with what they need. It is something that will make many others thank God. The way in which you have proved yourself by this service will bring honor and praise to God" (2 Cor. 9:12–13 CEV).

Day 27

My Heart to God's

God, a few days ago I didn't think much about my responsibility to minister and witness. Now I can hardly think of anything else.

People with needs are everywhere. Some in my town have lost jobs and don't have money for groceries or school supplies. Every day I hear of someone else who is seriously ill (not just older people). A girl in my school has leukemia, and two friends are in the hospital after a terrible accident. My next-door neighbor's son has just been sent to prison for drug dealing. And my home's not exactly perfect either.

I want to do my part, Lord. But where do I begin?

God's Heart to Mine

"Obey your parents in the Lord, for this is right. 'Honor your father and mother'—which is the first commandment with a promise" (Eph. 6:1–2).

"I will walk in my house with blameless heart" (Psalm 101:2).

Heart Thoughts

Katelyn is a leader at church and school. Most students consider her a model Christian teenager. She dresses stylishly but modestly, greets everyone with a smile, and encourages others to do their best.

But Katelyn at home is a different story. Her focus on herself and her sharp words to her brother prompt him to say, "If she's a Christian, I don't want to be one."

Ministry and witnessing should begin at home. Yet home is the hardest place to witness consistently. Why? Because at home we are really ourselves. In public we try to look and act our best; but at home we reveal the person within.[6] And if family members are not Christian believers, what we say and do is our witness to them.[7]

How can you minister and witness in your own home?

• Obey your parents, even when you disagree.

- Show consideration to each family member.
- Participate in a regular family devotion time. If there is none, ask your parents if you may begin mealtime devotions.[8]
- Pray for each family member by name.
- Express your love with hugs, smiles, and the words, "I love you."

By letting God's love flow through you, you reflect His light in your home.

My Heart's Prayer

Well, Lord, I'll be honest. My first thought is, "You don't know what it's like at my house. You don't know how unreasonable my parents can be." But You do know, don't You? I read about how Your parents didn't understand You when You were young either. But You obeyed them anyway.

So I'll start where You did, at home. Help me to be obedient, even when my parents _____.

I want to be kinder to my family, especially to _____ who's really been getting on my nerves. About family devotions, maybe we could start with learning a verse together each week. (We could even start with Eph. 6:1–2.)

Here's my Family Prayer List:

Name	Problem/Need	Spiritual Growth Need
_____	_____	_____
_____	_____	_____

I pray especially for _____ who has not yet trusted You as Savior. Please, Lord, love my family through me.

Heart Blessing

"May the God of peace . . . equip you with everything good for doing his will" (Heb. 13:20–21).

Day 28

My Heart to God's

Here I am again, Lord, waiting to learn more about ministry and witness for You. I'll admit I didn't expect You to say, "Start at home." (Though now it seems pretty obvious.)

I think You must love surprises. Do You have another in store for me today? As I meditate on other ways or places a teenaged girl like me can minister and witness in Your name, do it again, Lord! Surprise me!

God's Heart to Mine

"Let us draw near to God with a sincere heart. . . . And let us consider how we may spur one another on toward love and good deeds. Let us not give up meeting together, as some are in the habit of doing, but let us encourage one another" (Heb. 10:22,24–25).

Heart Thoughts

Jessica enjoys attending her Baptist church. One Sunday evening she brought her boyfriend, Michael, who was not a Christian. As the pastor preached earnestly, Michael listened attentively. But Jessica paid no attention to the sermon. Instead she wrote notes and whispered to her date. Soon Michael's attention shifted to Jessica. Her attitude during the worship service hindered him from hearing and heeding the gospel. A few weeks later, Michael's family moved. Neither Jessica nor her pastor ever had another opportunity to share God's good news with Michael.[9]

Above the doors of some churches are these words: "Enter to worship. Depart to serve." For followers of Christ, worship is both a privilege and a responsibility. The Scriptures teach that worshiping God publicly is important for each of us. And guess why nearly 90 percent of people come to church? Because they were influenced by friends![10] As faithful church attendance and reverent worship of

God nourish your personal relationship with Him, they give powerful evidence of your love for Him.

So do it—worship together at church, prepare yourself inside and out, spur each other on—see how creative you can be in encouraging love and helping others (Heb. 10:22–25, *author's paraphrase*). Learn from Jessica. Let your genuine worship overflow in ministry and witness!

My Heart's Prayer

Actually, God, I can identify with Jessica. Sometimes I've wasted opportunities for worshiping You, either by staying away from church or by being there physically but not mentally or spiritually. I, too, have whispered, giggled, drawn pictures, and written notes with church friends. Have I kept someone else from learning about Your love and trusting You?

The close connection between worship and service becomes clearer when I read in Luke 4:16–19 about Jesus worshiping. These words indicate that attending church was His habit:

_____.

The relationship of His worship to meeting people's needs is obvious in these phrases:

_____

_____.

I commit myself to developing worship habits more like Jesus did. To keep my worship focus on You, I will _____.
And I'll invite _____ to go with me this week.

Let my love for You and Your church shine, Lord!

Heart Blessing

"According to his power that is at work within us, to him be glory in the church and in Christ Jesus throughout all generations, for ever and ever! Amen" (Eph. 3:20–21).

Day 29

My Heart to God's

I'm beginning to get the picture, God—of where I should serve You. It's as if I am in the center of a circle that represents my home and family, and that's where serving begins. Around that circle is a larger one representing my church, also with opportunities for ministry and witness. Each circle of influence leads to another.

One thing is certain: No matter where it needs to happen, relating to others through ministry and witness is a challenge, Lord. But I like challenges! So what is the next one?

God's Heart to Mine

"Do not conform any longer to the pattern of this world, but be transformed by the renewing of your mind. Then you will be able to test and approve what God's will is—his good, pleasing and perfect will" (Rom. 12:2).

"Don't let anyone look down on you because you are young, but set an example for the believers in speech, in life, in love, in faith and in purity" (1 Tim. 4:12).

Heart Thoughts

Like a challenge? Try setting a Christlike example at school. A huge challenge, right? Here's why: The prevailing moral thought is "If it feels good, do it."[11] Add to that the peer pressure of "Everybody's doing it." No wonder it's harder than ever to be a witness at school.[12]

But school is where you touch lives with stressed teens like these: Jody, an anorexic, fixates on a self-image of being fat. Callie, caught up in the party scene, is into drinking. Mike takes steroids to excel as an athlete and win his dad's approval. Megan agonizes as her family is being torn apart by divorce. Consuela is failing English because her heart language is Spanish. Hurting, hopeless people you know struggle silently through these hardships.[13] They are all around you. They need the Lord. And you know Him!

What would happen if every teenaged Christian girl decided to be Christlike in every relationship at school? By offering friendship to hurting students, being honest on exams,[14] respecting each person, and demonstrating Christlike speech and conduct, you can shine Christ's light into their darkness.

So what's a challenge for?

My Heart's Prayer

I can't speak for every teenaged Christian girl, but I'd like to accept the challenge. I know I can't do it by myself because I've tried. But this time I'm trusting that You will work within me, providing Your strength and power exactly when I need it.

I'm listing here names of hurting people at school who need Your light in their lives. (Homeschoolers may list people within their field of influence.) Next I'll describe an action I can take to help meet that one's specific need.

Name	Need	Love in Action
_____	Self-image/Anorexic	_____
_____	Wants acceptance/Drinking	_____
_____	Wants to succeed/Takes drugs	_____
_____	Heartbroken/Divorce	_____
_____	Different culture/Isolated	_____
_____	Other	_____

Now I'll pray specifically for each one—and for an opportunity to show each Your love by my life. As I dare to be Your example at school, God, help me!

Heart Blessing

"May he work in us what is pleasing to him, through Jesus Christ, to whom be glory for ever and ever. Amen" (Heb. 13:21).

Day 30

My Heart to God's

After home, church, and school, I assume that the next arena for reflecting Your light is in my community. But there are many more people in that circle of influence, God. And I don't have a clue as to where to begin.

Should I start with the ones who live closest to me? Or should I start with a certain group of people? Or perhaps a certain kind of need? Or should I just try to show Your love to everyone You bring my way? Should I do the ministry by myself or with a group? This is beginning to be a little complex, and I'm not sure of the best plan.

How does one person make a difference in a whole community, God?

God's Heart to Mine

"'When I was hungry, you gave me something to eat, and when I was thirsty, you gave me something to drink. When I was a stranger, you welcomed me, and when I was naked, you gave me clothes to wear. When I was sick, you took care of me, and when I was in jail, you visited me.' . . . 'Whenever you did it for any of my people, no matter how unimportant they seemed, you did it for me'" (Matt. 25:35–36,40 CEV).

Heart Thoughts

As Mother Teresa took this teaching of Jesus to heart, she became a reflection of Christ's ministry and witness. Thinking of her service as ministering to the Lord Himself, Mother Teresa said, "We serve Jesus in the poor. We nurse Him, feed Him, clothe Him, visit Him, comfort Him in the poor, the abandoned, the sick, the orphans, the dying."[15] With a goal of proclaiming the gospel to "the poorest of the poor," this penniless woman founded a home for the dying, an orphanage, a leper colony, medical centers, and homeless shelters.[16]

Jesus' vivid parable of ministering to people in need teaches that His followers will be held accountable for our response to human need. He teaches that we must do what we can in our daily lives to meet persons' needs, and do so without calculating a reward. When we do, He considers that our help is given to Him.[17]

With God's help, ordinary people may relate to others as Jesus did—by meeting needs. Think of ministry as building a bridge to another's heart. Once the ministry bridge is built, you may walk across it to deliver the good news. The climax of ministry is helping another to know and love Jesus.

My Heart's Prayer

How incredible that You use ordinary people like me to reflect Your light in such simple ways, God! Anyone can give a meal to a hungry person, or a drink to a thirsty one, or welcome a stranger, cheer the sick, even visit a prisoner.[18]

The food pantry at church (or neighborhood) gives food in Christ's name to hungry families. I'll use some of my allowance to buy this for the pantry: _____.
I'll welcome a stranger (_____) at school by:

_____
I'll send a cheerful card to this sick friend: _____
I'll even "visit" a prisoner by writing a note to: _____.

Have I been overlooking these people? O God, forgive me. Open my eyes and ears to see them, and to hear their cries for help. Open my heart and hands to give help. Open my mouth to tell my story—and Yours!

Heart Blessing

"You, Lord God, bless everyone who cares for the poor, and you rescue those people in times of trouble. You protect them and keep them alive. You make them happy" (Psalm 41:1–2 CEV).

Day 31

My Heart to God's

God, more and more I'm excited about ministry. I receive so much joy from it. I think love in action is the best way to discover the joy of missions!

But I have a confession to make to You. I'm not so thrilled about witnessing. I'm just not very good at it. Sometimes I fear that friends will think I'm a religious freak and ridicule me. Many people think religion is too personal to discuss with others. And though I have no trouble talking about most other things, I feel timid talking about Jesus to my friends. I'm tempted to quit trying.[19] What should I do, Lord?

God's Heart to Mine

"'You are my witnesses'" (Luke 24:48).

"For what I received I passed on to you as of first importance: that Christ died for your sins according to the Scriptures, that he was buried, that he was raised on the third day. . . . But by the grace of God I am what I am, and his grace to me was not without effect" (1 Cor. 15:3–4,10).

Heart Thoughts

As a ten-year-old I felt guilty for disobeying my parents, telling lies, talking unkindly about classmates, and laughing at people different from me. And I was miserable! My next-door friend, Elizabeth, always seemed happy. One evening I mustered the courage to ask, "Your family is happy. What's the difference?"

"Jesus makes the difference," she said, "and He can make the difference for you!"

For weeks her words echoed in my ears. Then I trusted Christ at Vacation Bible School. "Jesus," I whispered, "I'm asking You to forgive my sins and make a difference in my life." And He did! He's been my friend, guide, strength, comfort, and joy ever since! That's my story.

Witnessing is telling your story, then telling His story. Your story includes (1) what your life was like before you trusted Christ; (2) what Christ did for you; and (3) what your life is like now. You are the expert at what God has done in your life.[20]

His story is the gospel: (1) Christ died for our sins. (2) Christ was buried. (3) Christ was raised from the dead. Our witness to Christ is that He accepts us as we are and makes a difference in our lives.[21]

What's your story?

My Heart's Prayer

God, I realize that I can't make someone say yes to You. But that's not my job, is it? My job is telling my story and Your story. (If a ten-year-old can witness, surely I can.) Today I'll write my story (testimony) here:

My life before trusting Christ:_____
_____.

What Jesus Christ did for me:_____
_____.

My life since trusting Christ:_____
_____.

I'll write Your story (gospel) here:

_____

_____

_____

Lord, lead me to someone I can witness to today.

Heart Blessing

"May our Lord Jesus Christ himself and God our Father, who loved us and by his grace gave us eternal encouragement and good hope, encourage your hearts and strengthen you in every good deed and word" (2 Thess. 2:16–17).

Day 32

My Heart to God's

O dear God, this week my eyes have been opened to see those who need Your love. I've begun to see some of them in my own family, some at church, others at school and still more in my community. I've been encouraged to minister to them in creative ways and then to share a witness of You and Your love.

Deep within, I want to influence others' lives just as people have influenced mine. As I continue to think about Jesus' servant example, I long to reach out to others with deeds and words that reflect Your light through ministry and witness.

How do I maintain this desire, Lord? Please, tell me how.

God's Heart to Mine

"But in your hearts set apart Christ as Lord. Always be prepared to give an answer to everyone who asks you to give the reason for the hope that you have. But do this with gentleness and respect" (1 Peter 3:15).

Heart Thoughts

Meet Jennifer (not her real name). This ordinary woman lives at risk in a Last Frontier country where openly sharing about Jesus is illegal. Only if someone asks may she talk about Him.

Jennifer ministers to prostitutes, women who trade sex for money in order to feed their families. During the daytime she visits these desperate women and gradually develops friendships. She asks about their families, problems, and interests. Occasionally she brings food or personal items. She expresses concern and offers help in time of sickness.

Eventually one will ask, "Why do you do this?" Then she tells them of Jesus, of His love for her—and for them. One by one, they trust Him as Savior. As they come out of that degrading lifestyle, Jennifer helps them to learn job skills to earn income while she teaches them God's word and helps them gain self-esteem. Her ministry is loving them in action. Her witness is telling them why.

Reaching out to unlovely persons will make you different from others. In a "me first" world of greed and hatred, people notice love. Look around you. Someone in your part of the world is desperate, needing Jesus' love. To whom will you minister until she asks, "Why?"

My Heart's Prayer

You've done it again, Lord. You've made me take a closer look at myself in light of Your word, Your example, and someone else's experience with You.

In my world are people who are avoided because of their appearance or their cultural background or their sin. Without You they are lost and hurting, and they are dying for lack of genuine love.

Who will I minister to until she asks, "Why?" I choose this person— this one who is shunned by others: _____.

This is the way I will begin to show Your love to her: _____ _____.

This is what I will say when she asks, "Why?" _____ _____.

May your love overflow out of my heart and life into hers, dear God.

Heart Blessing

"May the God of hope fill you with all joy and peace as you trust in him, so that you may overflow with hope by the power of the Holy Spirit" (Rom. 15:13).

5

Reflect Christ's Light in the World

Day 33

My Heart to God's

God, the more I read Your Word and pray about ministry and witness in Your name, the more I realize that it's not just for someone else. It's up close and personal, and it's part of my responsibility—and privilege!

But that's not the end of my responsibility and privilege, is it? The whole world is full of people with needs of every kind—physical, mental, emotional, and spiritual. Do You have a plan for all those people and needs? What is my specific part in Your big plan? How do I fit into that bigger picture, God?

God's Heart to Mine

"Again Jesus said, 'Peace be with you! As the Father has sent me, I am sending you'" (John 20:21).

Heart Thoughts

As a child, she was a prankster whom some classmates called Devil. But when Lottie Moon trusted Christ as Savior, she took seriously her commitment, serving almost 40 years as a missionary to China.

Her life was not easy. She struggled with language difficulties, discouragement, distrust, and loneliness. Still she stayed, teaching girls, evangelizing women, caring for sick and hungry—all while sharing Jesus' love. She took few furloughs (now stateside assignments) and refused to leave when famine struck China, though it meant starving to death. The avid letter writer once wrote, "I would I had a thousand lives that I might give them to the women of China."[1] Why? Because Lottie Moon had a mission:

A mission is one's destiny—what he is sent to do.[2] Mission is what gives meaning to life.[3]

Jesus had a mission: His first recorded words were "I *must be about my Father's business*" (Luke 2:49 KJV). He told His disciples that what sustained Him was doing "'*the will of the One who sent Me*'" (His mission) (John 4:34 *The Message*). His last words before dying on the Cross, "*It is finished*" (John 19:30), declare that He completed His earthly mission. And His legacy to His followers is to continue His mission.

In the Big Picture, every Christian has an on mission assignment: missionary or mission supporter. What is your mission?

My Heart's Prayer

I've often wondered why I am here, Lord—what I'm destined to do. You have sent me on a mission? Your mission? That's overwhelming, God. What is the mission You have in mind for me?

Am I to be a mission supporter—sharing Your light where I am by missions praying, missions giving, encouraging missionaries, and teaching younger girls about missions?
This is how I can serve You now as a mission supporter: _____
_____

Or do You want me to be a missionary—going to a specific place in another culture for a week, a month, or a lifetime to reflect Your loving light?

This is how I can prepare to serve You as a missionary in my country or another:_____

As I listen for Your direction, God, this is how I'm praying:_____
_____

Heart Blessing

"*How gracious he will be when you cry for help! . . . Whether you turn to the right or to the left, your ears will hear a voice behind you saying, 'This is the way; walk in it'*" (Isa. 30:19,21).

Day 34

My Heart to God's

As I continue to listen for Your direction, God, I'm thinking about my mission. I want to know more about my part in Your mission to bring people from every nation and tribe to faith in Jesus and worship of Him, but it seems like I'm in over my head.

In that Big Picture, what is Your strategy for reaching people from all nations? In a world where countless millions of people have never heard of Jesus or have no Bible in their language, how can one person make a difference? What kind of math is that? Help me understand, Lord.

God's Heart to Mine

"You have often heard me teach. Now I want you to tell these same things to followers who can be trusted to tell others" (2 Tim. 2:2 CEV).

Heart to Heart

Truly the world is so overflowing with people who don't know Jesus that it's hard to grasp. In fact, if the world's population lined up single file, the line would circle the globe 30 times, growing 20 miles longer daily.[4]

So what's God's strategy? Multiplication! God plans for us to not only be Jesus' disciples but to make disciples—not by adding, but by multiplying.[5]

Before ascending to heaven, Jesus delegated His responsibility to His followers in a plan called the Great Commission (Matt. 28:18–20). A commission grants authority and provides support for one person to act as an agent for another.[6]

After Jesus' ascension, Christians scattered rapidly to tell the good news in spite of persecution.[7] The Antioch church commissioned missionaries Paul and Barnabas, and mission supporters in churches helped with prayers and gifts. On mission Paul took

Timothy under his wing; Timothy discipled other faithful leaders who repeated the pattern.

Multiplication works. If each Christian led one person to Christ every six months, then each of those reached another, and so on, the world would be reached in 32 years.[8] That kind of multiplying is happening today in some areas of the world as twenty-first-century Christians reflect His light through the Great Commission.[9]

You do the math. Then follow His lead.

My Heart's Prayer

Amazing! Your multiplication strategy is truly amazing, God. One Person, Christ, started it, after all. And if each Christ follower keeps reaching others—even just two a year—Your plan will be complete in my lifetime.

So whether You ultimately call me to be a missionary in another culture or a mission supporter right where I am, my part in Your strategic plan is to help multiply Your followers. Therefore, I commit this to You: _____

_____

I thank You, God, for _____ who passed the torch of the gospel to me. Forgive me for not sharing the light of Your good news with these persons: _____

_____

Prepare their hearts as You work in mine. Open a door of opportunity to at least one of them that I may begin to multiply Your light into the world.

Heart Blessing

"Do everything without complaining or arguing, so that you may become blameless and pure, children of God without fault in a crooked and depraved generation, in which you shine like stars in the universe as you hold out the word of life" (Phil. 2:14–16).

Day 35

My Heart to God's

I see Your Great Commission in a new light, God. I intend to take it seriously. And it is obvious that if I'm to be a genuine multiplier of Christ followers, I'm going to need Your help.

But I'm beginning to consider this: Besides Your divine help, what are some of the job requirements of Great Commission Christians? What other qualifications do I need to have in order to reflect Your light into all the world?

God's Heart to Mine

"Only Jesus has the power to save! His name is the only one in all the world that can save anyone" (Acts 4:12 CEV).

"Jesus said to him, . . . 'For the Son of Man came to seek and to save what was lost'" (Luke 19:9–10).

Heart Thoughts

"Stay beside me," stressed Will's dad as the family entered the county fairgrounds. "Stay really close. In this big crowd you could get lost!"

"Yes, sir," answered the excited six-year-old as all his senses came alive. Will saw flashing lights of the Ferris wheel and merry-go-round. He heard laughter, and showmen calling, "Step right here!" He smelled popcorn and peanuts. He could almost taste cotton candy. He touched stuffed-animal prizes. Without realizing it, he followed his senses until . . . a strong hand grabbed his shoulder. Will turned to see his red-faced father.

"Where have you been?" cried his dad. "You've been gone an hour. Your mother and I have been frantic. You were lost!" And Will didn't even know it.

Most of the world's people are preoccupied with satisfying life's cravings and distracted by temptations. Countless millions without

Christ are lost to His loving forgiveness and all that is best for them. They are lost and don't even know it.

Great Commission Christians need conviction that people outside of Christ are lost in sin. Conviction is the strongest kind of belief, one that gives life a sense of urgency. Conviction of people's lostness compels us to reflect Christ's gospel light in the world before it is too late. Are you convicted?

My Heart's Prayer

God, I've been convicted of my own lostness before. That's when I came to know You personally, when I trusted You to forgive my sin and I accepted Your love gift of eternal life.

But I'll admit I haven't been thinking day and night about the lostness of other people. Thinking about what it means to be lost to Your love, and about how much of the world is lost without knowing it, makes me feel: _____

_____

_____

Sensing my need for a gripping conviction of the lost condition of people without Christ, this is my prayer: _____

_____

_____

Heart Blessing

"The same Lord is Lord of all and richly blesses all who call on him, for, 'Everyone who calls on the name of the Lord will be saved'" (Rom. 10:12–13).

Day 36

My Heart to God's

My conviction is growing, Lord. I have many friends who don't know You, who are headed for an eternity in darkness without You. My heart feels heavy as I realize that I am responsible for sharing Your light with them, one by one, and also for mentoring each one so that she may share with others.

Today, as I look for openings in my conversations to do this, I'm still pondering qualifications necessary for a Great Commission Christian. What else will help me to shine Your light into the world?

God's Heart to Mine

"During the night Paul had a vision of a man of Macedonia standing and begging him, 'Come over to Macedonia and help us.' After Paul had seen the vision, we got ready at once to leave for Macedonia, concluding that God had called us to preach the gospel to them" (Acts 16:9–10).

Heart Thoughts

My family calls it "the view from the top." While visiting New York City, our family gawked, wide-eyed at all the differences we southerners experienced. Sights, sounds, smells—everything was different. But most fascinating were the many different people—different colors, languages, clothes, and behavior.

When we went to the top of the Empire State Building, we viewed them all again. Only this time, we saw them very differently. From the top, everyone looked the same. We couldn't distinguish color, height, or weight; and we couldn't hear varied voices.

That's when my husband told our children: "Take a good look at the view from the top. This is God's view. When He looks at the world and all the people He made, He doesn't see differences. He sees hearts."

Vision is necessary for a Great Commission Christian. As physical vision requires light, so spiritual vision requires the Light of the world, Jesus. Christ followers reflect Christ's light in the world only when we regard the world and all its people from God's viewpoint.

When you look at God's world, what do you see? Do you see differences? Or do you see hearts?

My Heart's Prayer

I want Your vision, God—the "view from the top." I confess that my vision has been pretty dim. When I've looked at the world, I've seen differences: people with strange hair, facial features, clothes, and languages. Sometimes I've laughed at them; sometimes I've feared; sometimes I've hated—mostly because they are different.

But occasionally, when I've had glimpses of the world in Your light, here's what I've seen: stomachs bloated with malnutrition; weary, rag-covered bodies looking for a place to sleep; hearts painfully filled with hurts and needs; souls dying for love—Yours.

When I look at the world, will You help me see as You do? Give me Your vision, Lord. Looking at my world today, here's what I'm beginning to see:

Physical needs (hurts): _____

_____

Spiritual needs (hearts): _____

_____

Open the eyes of my heart, Lord!

Heart Blessing

"I pray also that the eyes of your heart may be enlightened in order that you may know the hope to which he has called you, the riches of his glorious inheritance in the saints, and his incomparably great power for us who believe" (Eph. 1:18–19).

Day 37

My Heart to God's

O dear God, since I asked for Your vision, I'm beginning to see people differently. More and more I view others according to their needs, both physical and spiritual. But something is happening to me in the process. Am I becoming different too?

I feel different, Lord. My heart seems heavy when I sense others' hurting hearts. What makes me feel like this? And what, if anything, does it have to do with reaching my world for You?

God's Heart to Mine

"Jesus called his disciples to him and said, 'I have compassion for these people'" (Matt. 15:32).

"Therefore, as God's chosen people, holy and dearly loved, clothe yourselves with compassion" (Col. 3:12).

Heart Thoughts

What drove Nancy and John Norton to Japan, half a world away from their family? What compelled this hearing couple to learn American and Japanese sign languages, in addition to speaking Japanese, in order to share God's love? Compassion for the Deaf peoples in Japan who need to know Jesus cares for them.

What caused Kay Bennett to go to the often dangerous and unpredictable inner city of New Orleans, Louisiana? What keeps her working day and night to provide safe shelter, hot meals, decent clothing, and a glimmer of hope to street people? Compassion for homeless women and children who need the security and warmth of Jesus' love.

What made Mike leave a growing business in the United States and start a new business in a land of suspicious strangers? What drives him to remain in that Last Frontier country where his life and other believers' lives are at high risk of persecution or death?

Compassion for Muslim peoples who have never felt the love of Jesus.

Reflecting Christ's light in our dark world requires compassion. Compassion is having His heartache for all people—His sorrow for suffering and great urge to help. A Great Commission Christian's heart aches for all people to know Christ. Does your heart ache?

My Heart's Prayer

Is that what I feel, Lord? Could my heartache be the beginning of compassion? That's scary. When I think about the Nortons and Kay and Mike having compassion and where You sent them, I get nervous.

Forgive me, God, for thinking about my comfort zone. Help me to care less about my heart's hurting and more about hearts who don't know You. Give me Your kind of passion for people everywhere, no matter where that may lead.

As I look at Your world through the windows of television newscasts or daily newspapers, my heart aches for people living in darkness within this culture: _____

_____

Here is my prayer for them:_____

_____

And for myself I pray:_____

_____

Heart Blessing

"Because of the Lord's great love we are not consumed, for his compassions never fail. They are new every morning; great is your faithfulness" (Lam. 3:22–23).

Day 38

My Heart to God's

It's me, Lord, calling on You again. I've heard my pastor and some missionaries tell how You called them to a certain kind of Christian service. I wonder about Your call.

What does it mean to be "called"? Who are the special ones whom You call? How old must people be when You call them? How does a person answer Your call?

Does a Great Commission Christian need to be called by You, God?

God's Heart to Mine

"Then the Lord called Samuel. . . . The Lord came and stood there, calling as at the other times, 'Samuel! Samuel!' Then Samuel said, 'Speak, for your servant is listening'" (1 Sam. 3:4,10).

"The angel of the Lord appeared to him in flames of fire from within a bush. . . . When the Lord saw that he had gone over to look, God called to him from within the bush, 'Moses, Moses!' And Moses said, 'Here I am'" (Ex. 3:2,4).

Heart Thoughts

I heard of a mother who was watching television with her three-year-old daughter Emily when a newsman announced the death of a famous person. "Is he going to heaven?" asked Emily.

"Yes, if he invited Jesus to live in his heart as Savior," said her mom.

"I talked to Jesus on the phone," Emily declared, "and I asked Him to come into my heart."

"That's great," said her mom, "but how did you know His number?"

Emily replied, "He called me!"

Emily's profound answer is our challenge today. He calls me and you and every Christ follower to reflect His light in His world.

The Scriptures reveal that God has always called people, whether bashful or bold, young or old. God's call to Samuel, Moses, and others teaches that God is always calling. His call is personal, specific, and comes in different ways and places. He may call us to share His love right where we are or across the ocean. And He always equips us to do what He calls us to do.

Great Commission Christians listen expectantly for God's call and answer with faithfulness.

My Heart's Prayer

You're calling me, God? I don't feel worthy of being called by You. I have few strengths and many weaknesses; I'm not quite grown and still in school. But compared to You, I guess no one is worthy.

Forgive me for ignoring when You may have called before. I have felt Your presence nudging my heart at other times, such as when I:_____

_____

I sense Your still, small voice speaking in my heart now. God, I believe You may be calling me to do this some day: _____

_____

I think You're calling me to do this now: _____

_____

Here I am, Lord, willing to answer Your call.

Heart Blessing

"We constantly pray for you, that our God may count you worthy of his calling, and that by his power he may fulfill every good purpose" (2 Thess. 1:11).

Day 39

My Heart to God's

God, I'm serious about wanting to be what You created me to be. I want to answer Your call, whether it leads to some remote corner of the earth or across the street. I'm awed by Bible people—like Philip and Paul, Timothy and Luke—among the first to obey Your Great Commission.

But that was long ago in a very different world. When I think of all that's required, I have to wonder: *How is it still possible to be a Great Commission Christian in today's world?*

God's Heart to Mine

"'But you will receive power when the Holy Spirit comes on you; and you will be my witnesses in Jerusalem, and in all Judea and Samaria, and to the ends of the earth'" (Acts 1:8).

Heart Thoughts

Single Susan is average size and weight, wears glasses, and speaks softly. Though not allowed to speak openly of Jesus, she glows with His love as she teaches college English in the faraway Last Frontier. Seeking the secret of her happiness, students come to her apartment where they discover Jesus' love.

With her large frame and commanding voice, Sheila is impressive. This wife and mom serves in a shelter for homeless women and children. She sweats as she cooks, keeps books, soothes scraped knees and wounded hearts, helps abused women find jobs, and loves them to Jesus.

Petite, ever-smiling Tina resembles Peter Pan as children follow her everywhere. Though plagued with health problems, she teaches children to cook African food, sing at nursing homes, and give to missions. At camp, Tina's face radiates God's love as she trains the next generation of missionaries.

My three friends are different ages, sizes, and colors, serving in different ways and places. Yet they are much alike.

Each is on mission with God, multiplying disciples. Convicted that multitudes are lost without Jesus, each views people's heart needs as God does, and has compassion for a specific group of people to know Jesus. Each is answering God's call.

These are Great Commission Christians! Are you?

My Heart's Prayer

O dear God, it is possible for a person to be a Great Commission Christian today. These are ordinary people with extraordinary love for You. That means it is possible even for me to follow Your Great Commission—with Your help, of course.

Of the qualities needed for carrying out Your Commission, I feel stronger in some than others, and especially weak in some. Help me honestly assess my strengths and weaknesses by writing how I feel about them here:

My mission with You:_____

_____

My multiplying of disciples: _____

_____

My conviction of people's lost condition without Jesus: _____

_____

My view of other persons: _____

_____

My compassion for a specific group of people:_____

_____

My call from God:_____

_____

Heart Blessing

"And I pray that you, being rooted and established in love, may have power . . . to grasp how wide and long and high and deep is the love of Christ . . . that you may be filled to the measure of all the fullness of God" (Eph. 3:17–19).

Day 40

My Heart to God's

God, when I started this devotional book, 40 days seemed like a long time. But 40 days is a short time to develop lifelong habits of a Christ follower.

My quiet time of reflecting on You and Your word through prayer and Bible study helps me all day long. Journaling clarifies my thoughts and feelings. I'm learning to respond to Your love by responsible giving as well as by ministry and witnessing.

I don't want this to stop, Lord. How can I keep growing—and glowing—in this Christlike lifestyle?

God's Heart to Mine

"'Arise, shine, for your light has come, and the glory of the Lord rises upon you. . . . Nations will come to your light, and kings to the brightness of your dawn. . . . Then you will look and be radiant, your heart will throb and swell with joy; . . . for the Lord will be your everlasting light'" (Isa. 60:1,3,5,19).

"'And surely I am with you always'" (Matt. 28:20).

Heart Thoughts

College sophomore Jenni sent these email messages while on a summer missions trip to Africa:

"At first I was homesick. Then I remembered God's promise to be with me always. I feel His presence here."

"We started ministry today; I'm excited to use my gifts for God's purpose! The AIDS-stricken children are responsive to God's word."

"All the children are precious, but Iwo has captured my heart. With his haunting dark eyes and snaggletoothed grin, he follows me everywhere. . . . There is something about this place that is indescribable. . . . Though far away from home, with the peace of the Lord there is no need to fear."

The Great Commission includes a promise. Wherever God calls you to serve Him, He will be with you. Always.

Have you felt His nearness while reflecting on Him, His Word, and His world?

Consider repeating this devotional journal for the next 40 days, writing in another color. Join your accountability partner to help you continue:

> reflecting with Christ through prayer;
> reflecting on Christ through Bible study;
> reflecting Christ's light by sharing your blessings;
> reflecting Christ's light through ministry and witness; and
> reflecting Christ's light in the world.

Arise, shine! He is with you. Always.

My Heart's Prayer

Yes, Lord, I feel You're with me now. And I love You, God, because:

_____

Forgive my many failed attempts at genuine prayer and Bible study. Help me make time with You my priority by:

_____

Help me use my resources of time, talents, money, and influence more responsibly by:

_____

Help me overcome fear as I minister and witness in Your name to:

_____

Help me to hear and answer Your call, and to personalize Your Great Commission by:

_____

Forgive my failure to reflect Your light in the world. Whatever it takes, Lord, please shine through me.

Heart Blessing

"'The Lord bless you and keep you; the Lord make his face shine upon you and be gracious to you; the Lord turn his face toward you and give you peace'" (Num. 6:24–26).

Notes

Section 1

[1]Billy K. Smith, *Never Alone* (Nashville: Broadman Press, 1978), 60.

[2]Ibid.

[3]Ibid.

[4]David Allan Hubbard, *The Practice of Prayer: A Guide for Beginners* (Downers Grove, IL: InterVarsity Press, 1983), 19.

[5]Ibid., 24.

[6]Ruth Harms Calkin, *Lord, You Love to Say Yes* (Elgin, IL: David C. Cook Publishing Co., 1981), 46.

[7]Rosalie Beck, ed., *Mildred McMurry's Spiritual Life Development: Her Classic Volume Revisited* (Birmingham, AL: Woman's Missionary Union, 1994), 63.

[8]Hubbard, *The Practice of Prayer*, 27.

[9]Calkin, *Lord, You Love to Say Yes*, 20.

Section 2

[1]Nikolai Alexandrenko, professor emeritus, Louisiana College, Louisiana Baptist Convention, Pineville, Louisiana, telephone interview with author, March 13, 2003.

[2]Janet T. Hoffman, *God Is Calling You: And Other Things My Granddad Taught Me* (Birmingham, AL: New Hope Publishers, 2002), 22–23.

[3]Ibid., 23.

[4]As cited in Paul W. Powell, *Joy Comes in the Morning* (Dallas: Texas Baptist Leadership Center, Inc., Baptist General Convention of Texas, n.d.), 71.

[5]For more information on True Love Waits, visit www.truelovewaits.com.

[6]Kathryn Ellen Carpenter, telephone interview with author for monologue used in Louisiana WMU Centennial Celebration, March 1998.

[7]Bill Fudge, "Preachables," vol. 35 (March 3, 2003), email transmission.

[8]Last Frontier missionary speaking to WMU, SBC, Executive Board Meeting, Talladega, Alabama, January 12, 2003.

Section 3

[1]Author unknown, *The Baptist Record*, February 20, 2003.

[2]Edith Kirkpatrick, "Acknowledging My Stewardship," in *Star Ideals* (Birmingham, AL: Woman's Missionary Union, [1963]), 73.

[3]Ibid.

[4]William Barclay, *The Gospel of Matthew*, rev. ed. (Philadelphia: Westminster Press, 1975), 2:329–30.

[5]William Barclay, *The Gospel of Mark*, rev. ed. (Philadelphia: Westminster Press, 1975), 302.

[6]As cited in Cathy Butler, *With Willing Hands: Living in Harmony with God's Plan* (Birmingham, AL: Woman's Missionary Union, 2003), 31.

[7]Paul W. Powell, *Taking the Stew Out of Stewardship* (Dallas: Annuity Board of the Southern Baptist Convention, 1996), 129.

[8]Charles Lowery, "Fireproofing," SBC *Life* 10, no. 10 (September 2002) [journal online]; available from http://www.sbclife.org/articles/2002/09/sla10.asp; Internet; accessed November 24, 2003.

[9]William Barclay, *The Gospel of Matthew*, rev. ed. (Philadelphia: Westminster Press, 1975), 1:122–23.

[10]Ibid., 125.

[11]Ibid., 122.

[12]Elizabeth M. Hoekstra, *A Heart After God* (Minneapolis: Bethany House Publishers, 2002), 75–76.

[13]As cited in Powell, *Taking the Stew Out of Stewardship*, 35.

[14]Ibid., 76.

[15]Kirkpatrick, "Acknowledging My Stewardship," 75.

Section 4

[1]Cindy Townsend, Women's Missions and Ministries director, Louisiana Baptist Convention, Alexandria, Louisiana, interview with author, August 7, September 11, 2003.

[2]As cited in Paul W. Powell, *Dynamic Discipleship* (Nashville: Broadman Press, 1984), 80.

[3]As cited in Joanne Stuart Sloan and Cheryl Sloan Wray, *A Life That Matters: Spiritual Disciplines That Change the World* (Birmingham, AL: New Hope Publishers, 2002), 189.

[4]William Barclay, *The Gospel of John*, rev. ed. (Philadelphia: Westminster Press, 1975), 2:141.

[5]Oswald Chambers, *My Utmost for His Highest* (Westwood, NJ: Barbour and Company, Inc., 1963), 255.

[6]Powell, *Dynamic Discipleship*, 116–17.

[7]Floy Barnard, "Adorning Myself with Good Works," in *Star Ideals* (Birmingham, AL: Woman's Missionary Union, [1963]), 98–99.

[8]Ibid., 100.

[9]Adapted from Barnard, "Adorning Myself with Good Works," 103.

[10]Woodrow Kroll, "The Exercise of Witnessing," *Back to the Bible* radio broadcast, April 24, 2003; available from http://www.backtothebible.org/radio/today/23616; Internet; accessed November 21, 2003.

[11]Powell, *Dynamic Discipleship*, 112.

[12]Ibid.

[13]Adapted from Leo Endel, "People Need the Lord!" article in State Missions Season of Prayer Packet (Rochester, MN: Minnesota-Wisconsin Baptist Convention, 2003).

[13]Barnard, "Adorning Myself with Good Works," 105–6.

[15]As cited in Joanne Stuart Sloan and Cheryl Sloan Wray, *A Life That Matters: Spiritual Disciplines That Change the World* (Birmingham, AL: New Hope Publishers, 2002), 180.

[16]Ibid., 179.

[17]William Barclay, *The Gospel of Matthew*, rev. ed. (Philadelphia: Westminster Press, 1975), 2:325–26.

[18]Ibid., 325.

[19]Barnard, "Adorning Myself with Good Works," 117.

[20]Powell, *Dynamic Discipleship*, 82.

[21]Ibid., 83.

Section 5

[1]Catherine B. Allen, *The New Lottie Moon Story*, 2nd ed. (Birmingham, AL: Woman's Missionary Union, 1980), 175.

[2]Rick Warren, *The Purpose-Driven Life* (Grand Rapids, MI: Zondervan, 2002), 281–82.

[3]Ibid., 285.

[4]Paul W. Powell, *Dynamic Discipleship* (Nashville: Broadman Press, 1984), 99.

[5]Ibid., 99–100.

[6]Saxon Rowe Carver, "Accepting the Challenge of the Great Commission," in *Star Ideals* (Birmingham, AL: Woman's Missionary Union, [1963]), 124.

[7]Ibid., 130–31.

[8]Powell, *Dynamic Discipleship*, 100.

[9]Jerry Rankin, "Date with Destiny," Missionary Appointment Service (Virginia Beach, VA; London Bridge Baptist Church; July 13, 2003); and Bill Fudge, "Preachables," vol. 36 (March 22, 2003), email transmission.